AN INTEGRAL APPROACH TO CREATING SUSTAINABLE PROSPERITY

A JOURNEY TO SPIRITUAL AND MATERIAL ABUNDANCE THROUGH YOUR OWN PERSONAL AND COLLECTIVE EXPERIENCE

DORIS G. HOSKINS MA

SEPTEMBER 2017

copyrighted 2013, 8th printing

Table of Contents

An Integral Approach to:

Creating Sustainable

Prosperity!

Table of Contents

Dedication:

This book is dedicated to my children, my grandchildren, and all of those to whom I have taught prosperity over the years. It is especially dedicated to the late Nancy Smith, Founding President of the Leadership Council of Unity of Northern Kentucky, and the entire Congregation of Unity of Northern Kentucky without whom this book would never have been written.

The following is quoted from an email with permission:

On Dec 28, 2016, at 9:50 AM, Reverend Joanne Rowden wrote:

Hi Doris,

…Blessed Christmas to you! I finally had a few moments to respond…

I found Sustainable Prosperity to be a great success in our ministry.

I had 15 individuals complete the full year study.

Of those 15, 9 have signed up to do it again in 2017! That alone speaks to the power of the class. Several people who dropped out last year for various reasons have signed back up again. All who completed the class experienced wonderful shifts in their prosperity consciousness. All agreed the intentions that they began the class with were fulfilled through the course of the year. I am offering the class again for 2017…

I am so grateful for this class. Thank you so much Doris.

Abundant peace and blessings…

Joanne

Acknowledgments

While the Bibliography will include all of the books that I have used I particularly want to acknowledge Unity Publishing for allowing me to use a chapter from Eric Butterworth's *Spiritual Economics,* and from Emilie Cady's *Lesson's in Truth.* I also want to acknowledge David Friedman for allowing me to use his wonderful booklet, *Is Tithing For Me?* The work of Jacob Needleman's *Money and the Meaning of Life* and Suzie Ormond's *The 9 Steps to Financial Freedom* are also an important part of this book.

I also owe much to my son Jeffrey Hoskins for his help in editing this book and my friend, the late Nancy Smith, for helping me for many days to do a final read through. Thanking you both with all my love always.

INTRODUCTION

Beginning with the concept that led Ken Wilbur to his Integral Theory," no one is ever 100 percent wrong," I wanted to identify and then synthesize all that I have learned over the years from the many teachers and authors who have crossed my spiritual and academic path, thoroughly laying the groundwork for a new and distinct Integral Theory of Prosperity.

My gift is seeing things in a way that others do not seem to see them. My Harmony Pendant does not have anything original in it. It is simply my vision and how I composed it back in 1998 that is different from other variations that you may have seen on bumper stickers, in the media or on a piece of jewelry. The arrangement of the various symbols makes it unique and copyrightable. The same is true of the information in this book. I am borrowing from others who have talked about, and taught about, money, prosperity.

What is different is how I see the individual pieces fitting together. That is the uniqueness that I have to offer the world. To take what is and see it differently, whether in a house, a symbol, or a person, I see a potential that exists fully before me, already manifested. That does not mean that it will not take a great deal of work to make it so… It can be as short as hours or weeks, or, more likely than not, it may even take months, and, possibly, years.

I have been a part of a movement that has taught prosperity, in various manifestations, since Unity's founding in the late 19th century. I have practiced and taught these concepts for nearly 30 years; over twenty as an Ordained Unity Minister. I know all the ways that prosperity, as taught by Unity, work. I have demonstrated the ways that it works in my own life many times since I began to tithe back in the late 1980's, and I have also found the ways that prosperity as we teach it does not work. It is my observation that in many instances the principles by themselves have not been enough to sustainably benefit Unity Village's or Unity World Wide's income statement, and, accordingly, the hundreds of individual churches within the movement, and the numerous ministers who lived and worked near or at the poverty level while supposedly teaching prosperity. Working from that premise, I believe Wilber's contention that prosperity as we have taught it is not wrong—it is simply insufficient. The same has been true of other books about financial literacy and prosperity that I have read, and teachers to whom I have listened and from whom I have learned. This is my attempt to put their teachings together in a different way, and see if it works—first of all for me, then for others who take this class and practice its premises. Ultimately, it is my hope and intention that some of the prosperity principles as taught in Unity are further amended in this way.

Writing a course about prosperity is one of the very last things that I ever expected to do. I have taken and taught prosperity classes over the course of twenty years as a Unity minister. I believe that I have taught every class that is popular in the Unity Movement, from Charles Fillmore and Stretton Smith, to Edwine Gaines, Katherine Ponder, Diane Harmony, David Owen Ritz, Mary Morrissey and last, but certainly not least, to Eric Butterworth and his *Spiritual Economics*.

In creating the suggested bylaws for Unity of Northern Kentucky the steering team made the decision that a prosperity class would be a requirement for all members. The question became, what class would be the first one taught? In reviewing the possibilities, and meditating on what each had to offer, I found that there were elements that were missing for me in each one. In the past I have also used Suze Orman for teaching some of the practical aspects of how to deal effectively with individual and collective finances. I then remembered my work with the concepts that I learned from Maria Nemeuth. I began to wonder why a class did not exist that combined the teachings of Truth and the practical aspects of managing money. I also began to wonder why, when Unity does not interpret the Bible literally, why the only verse in the Bible that we do take literally is Malachi 3:10, *"Bring the whole tithe into the storehouse, that there may be food in my house. Test me in this," says the LORD Almighty, "and see if I will not throw open the floodgates of heaven and pour out so much blessing that you will not have room enough for it."* The whole third chapter of Malachi is devoted to tithing. The verses that we use in this context are Malachi 3:6-12 (NIV):

> *"⁶I the Lord do not change. So you, the descendants of Jacob, are not destroyed. ⁷ Ever since the time of your ancestors you have turned away from my decrees and have not kept them. Return to me, and I will return to you," says the Lord Almighty. "But you ask, 'How are we to return?'⁸ "Will a mere mortal rob God? Yet you rob me. "But you ask, 'How are we robbing you?' "In tithes and offerings. ⁹ You are under a curse—your whole nation—because you are robbing me. ¹⁰ Bring the whole tithe into the storehouse, that there may be food in my house. Test me in this," says the Lord Almighty, "and see if I will not throw open the floodgates of heaven and pour out so much blessing that there will not be room enough to store it. ¹¹ I will prevent pests from devouring your crops, and the vines in your fields will not drop their fruit before it is ripe," says the Lord Almighty. ¹² "Then all the nations will call you blessed, for yours will be a delightful land," says the LordAlmighty.*

Are we really suggesting that individuals who do not tithe are robbing God? Are we suggesting that they are robbing our church? Or are we suggesting that those who do not tithe are robbing us? How about Jesus' teaching about tithing? Looking in the books of the Christian Bible we read Jesus' only teaching about tithing in Luke 18: 9- 14 (NIV) we read:

The Parable of the Pharisee and the Tax Collector

> *⁹ To some who were confident of their own righteousness and looked down on everyone else, Jesus told this parable: ¹⁰ "Two men went up to the temple to pray, one a Pharisee and the other a tax collector. ¹¹ The Pharisee stood by himself and prayed: 'God, I thank you that I am not like other people—robbers, evildoers, adulterers—or even like this tax collector. ¹² I fast twice a week and give a tenth of all I get.' ¹³ "But the tax collector stood at a distance. He would not even look up to heaven, but beat his breast and said, 'God, have mercy on me, a sinner.' "¹⁴ I tell you that this man, rather than the other, went home justified before God. For all those who exalt themselves will be humbled, and those who humble themselves will be exalted."*

Then there are the parallel teachings of the"8 woes" in **Matthew 23:22-24** and **Luke 11:41-43** (NIV):

Matthew [22] *And anyone who swears by heaven swears by God's throne and by the one who sits on it.* [23] *"Woe to you, teachers of the law and Pharisees, you hypocrites! You give a tenth of your spices—mint, dill and cumin. But you have neglected the more important matters of the law—justice, mercy and faithfulness. You should have practiced the latter, without neglecting the former.* [24] *You blind guides! You strain out a gnat but swallow a camel.*

Luke11: [41] *But now as for what is inside you—be generous to the poor, and everything will be clean for you.* [42] *"Woe to you Pharisees, because you give God a tenth of your mint, rue and all other kinds of garden herbs, but you neglect justice and the love of God. You should have practiced the latter without leaving the former undone.* [43] *"Woe to you Pharisees, because you love the most important seats in the synagogues and respectful greetings in the marketplaces.*

However, the word tithe is used twenty-nine times in the Hebrew Bible. Let's look to the dictionary for a definition of tithe:

"Contribution of a tenth of one's income for religious purposes. The practice of tithing was established in the Hebrew Scriptures and was adopted by the Western Christian church. It was enjoined by ecclesiastical law from the 6th century and enforced in Europe by secular law from the 8th century. After the Reformation, tithes continued to be imposed for the benefit of both the Protestant and Roman Catholic churches. Tithes were eventually repealed in France (1789), Ireland (1871), Italy (1887), and England (1936). In Germany support for churches is collected through the personal income tax and distributed according to the individual's religious affiliation. Tithing was never part of U.S. law, but members of certain churches are required to tithe, and members of other churches may tithe voluntarily. Tithing was never accepted by the Eastern Orthodox churches."
Merriam Webster http://www.merriam-webster.com/concise/tithe?show=0&t=1361235558

I also want to be perfectly clear. I tithe now. I have tithed since 1990, except for an eight-month period in 2006 when I bought a condo that would further allow me to simplify my life, expecting my house to sell in a timely manner. At the time I stopped tithing, I had two mortgages, two sets of utilities, and housing expenses that amounted to 98% of my take-home pay; I subsequently went into fear and stopped tithing. When I realized I was being driven by fear and lack, and wrote two tithe checks to the individuals who helped me remember The Truth, my condo immediately sold, which allowed me to move back into my house and once again to reduce my expenses. So, I recognize the benefits of tithing and yet I have watched it become a "magic charm" that if used will restore the necessary cash flow to one's life. It fails as a "magic charm".

As I stated earlier, one of the truths that I have learned from my studies of the work of Ken Wilbur is that nothing is ever 100 percent wrong. As I spent weeks meditating and reflecting on the combined concept I was in the process of reading Paul Smith's *Integral Christianity*. My master's degree is in Organizational Management with an emphasis in Integral Studies. Thinking about prosperity I began to wonder if an Integral Approach to prosperity was the answer that I was looking for. In looking into the Christian Bible what I found in Jesus' teachings was an emphasis on giving. He did not suggest or recommend tithing. We in Unity have always taught that prosperity was more than money. We have taught that prosperity was about true abundance in our lives. Namely, that we are entitled to abundance in everything—meaningful relationships, friendships, health, experiences, and even life itself—to have "more than enough" of everything that we require to have a wonderful and whole life.

I know that when appearances tell me that, "I do not have enough money," and I write my tithe check anyway, the money to pay my bills somehow will miraculously appear. Therefore, why am I reluctant to simply use one of the courses that I have taught before? Because… during my ministry I have watched individuals in my class write tithe checks when they were living on credit cards. I have watched them celebrate because they had received a new credit card in the mail. I've watched them spend money that they did not have to buy things they did not need or want, all because that made them "feel prosperous" and I have watched them go bankrupt while continuing to tithe.

I wanted to take the good that comes from generous giving and combine that with the practicality of good money management that will provide them with a sustainable prosperity. I wanted to give them a blue print for living prosperously and a blue print for managing money that includes the practicality and reality of effectively budgeting, saving, and investing. I wanted to find for myself and others how our shadow contexts for money affect our whole lives. I wanted to bring an integral practice to our finances. This is the course I created that I now offer

An Integral Approach to:

Creating Sustainable Prosperity

Chapter 1

It's Not About Tithing

Spending Record

INSTRUCTIONS:

Over the course of the next six weeks, these instructions will apply to the weekly exercise:

In order to receive the full benefits of this course it is important to look at exactly how, when, and where you spend your money, while gaining a full understanding of leakage points in your finances. Some of you never really count the dollars that you spend. For some of you simply signing your name (or not if making an online transaction) to a credit card slip, whether debit or credit, is so easy that you never actually notice the funds draining from your banking, credit card, or investment accounts.

After six weeks you will completely understand where your money goes. Please understand that I am not here to tell you literally how to spend your hard-earned money, but rather to have you take a closer look at **How** you spend your money on a daily basis – namely, if **How** you actually spend your money is really a reflection of your core values and, therefore, necessary **or** important to you. Please give your careful attention to doing these weekly exercises as precisely as possible. Giving thoughtful attention to **What Is** the first step to creating what you want to have. This concept is a practical aspect of what Charles Fillmore, co-founder of Unity, calls **Denials and Affirmations**. We will understand what we do and what we do not do with our eyes wide open, so that we can affirm, with **Attending Action**, what we actually want to create in our lives.

Cash Management:

The first part of the exercise is to record our cash on hand, to the penny. **This "big count" need happen only once if you are carefully keeping track of cash that comes in and cash that goes out.** This big count will start with the cash in your wallet, purse, or billfold and will include all of the cash you have "stashed" in various places in your home, all of the change you throw in a jar in your home you throw change into, and the money that lays in your car for tolls, or parking meters. Enter that amount on the top line. Record any cash that you acquire from an ATM, cash payment of some kind that is made to you, refunds, or even money you find on the street. Then you will record each purchase you make using cash. Total accounting is required, from coffee at your favorite beverage stop, to parking meters, tips received, and money given as hand-outs—every penny! Then you will add it all together at the end of each week.

For the second part of this weekly assignment, please also record whether the purchase was an essential purchase (need) or a non-essential purchase (want). I invite you to notice if this decision, whether something is either essential or non-essential, changes as the weeks pass. For example, you may consider morning coffee at your local coffee shop as an essential item. However, as you write it down repeatedly over the coming weeks, you may decide that making coffee at home more often, rather than buying it out, can shift that purchase from essential to non-essential.

The second part is to record all non-cash transactions, be they credit card purchases, checks written, bank transfers, or bills paid online. This will include paying your monthly bills. Obviously the week you pay your rent or your mortgage you will have bigger totals. Again, we just want to get everything on paper so that we can take a look at it.

In the first class I taught, I was asked why I did not want to have students record their income with this work. My experience has taught me that most spending does not happen in the context of what we earn. It falls into the category of what we *Want* (non-essential) versus what we *Need* (essential). Hence the reason for looking at whether the expenditure is we *Want* or *Need.* I invite you to look closely at this distinction over the coming weeks. It is part of the key to this class.

End your week the *Night Before* your class so that you can do the totals and work before you come to class. Be sure to include the day of your class in the coming week.

The **VERY IMPORTANT** part of the weekly assignment is to journal about what you noticed as you do these assignments each week. Don't hold back whatever comes up for you. Your resistance, your anger your amazement at where your money actually goes. How having to keep track of what you spend feels.

TIPS FROM THOSE WHO HAVE GONE BEFORE YOU!

- **ASK FOR AND KEEP EVERY RECEIPT FOR EVERYTHING YOU SPEND. TRYING TO RECONSTRUCT WHAT YOU SPEND AND WHERE AFTER THE FACT WILL JUST DRIVE YOU CRAZY AND IT WON'T WORK. EVEN WRITING ON THE RECEIPT SO THAT YOU KNOW WHAT IT WAS FOR MAY HELP LATER.**
- **DOING THIS WORK IN PENCIL WILL MAKE YOUR LIFE MUCH EASIER AS WILL HAVING A GOOD ERASER.**
- **YOU WILL COME AND GO IN THIS BOOK, SOME STICKY NOTE TABS MAY HELP YOU MOVE AROUND EASIER IN THE BOOK.**
- **THIS WORK CAN'T ALL BE DONE THE NIGHT BEFORE.**

WEEK 1:_____, date

How much cash do you have in your wallet? (To the penny)   _____

Add in any cash you had at home, or in your car, as of this date: _____

Beginning Total =   _____

Any payment received in cash this week — for what:

_____

_____

How much?   _____

Number of trips to ATM?   _____

Other sources for cash?   _____

Amount of additional cash withdrawn this week?   _____

Total Cash for Week =   _____

List of cash purchases for the week: This means every purchase. A can of soda, parking meters, gum, coffee. If you spent a penny write it down. Occasion for purchase might be: essential, non-essential...wanted, needed, bored, everyone else was...

PURCHASE	AMOUNT	OCCASION FOR PURCHASE
_____	_____	_____
_____	_____	_____
_____	_____	_____
_____	_____	_____
_____	_____	_____
_____	_____	_____
_____	_____	_____
_____	_____	_____
_____	_____	_____
_____	_____	_____
_____	_____	_____
_____	_____	_____

Total Amount Spent this Week: _____

Funds on Hand at the End of Week: _____

NON-CASH EXPENDITURES:

PURCHASE	AMOUNT	WANT...NEED?

Total Non-Cash Expenditures this Week: $_____

Total Cash Expenditures this Week $_____

Total Weekly Expenditure $_____

LOOKING AT THIS WEEKS EXPENDITURES

Number of trips to the grocery store:_____   Amount spent: _____

Look at the individual items purchased at the grocery store. Are there items that are personal to you and not really food related?_____Should these items be part of your food budget?_____Notice pre-packaged items, pre-made items, i.e. frozen dinners, pizzas, canned food you simply open and heat, time saving foods. Simply notice how much you would save if you purchased fresh ingredients and made from scratch and added your own spices, etc. Lots of money is spent on groceries that is no longer eaten but are called "groceries" nevertheless. Notice any reactions:

_____

Number of meals eaten out_____By yourself_____With others_____Amount spent_____

Entertainment_____   Self_____   Family_____Amount spent_____
          (*This would include movies, books, plays, ballgames, clubs, hobbies, toys, etc.*)

Personal Care _____   Self_____   Family_____Amount spent_____
          (*This would include haircuts, massages, toiletry items, mani—pedi, medications, etc.*)

Clothing_____Self_____   Family_____Amount spent_____
          (*Notice if this was an intentionally pre-planned purchase or on an impulse. Was it needed, Wanted? Were you alone or with someone else?*)

Household items_____Individual purchase_____Family purchase_____Amount spent_____
(Mortgage, rent, insurance, major purchase, knick-knacks, cleaning supplies or contracted services, etc.)

Automobile Related_____Individual Car_____Family Member_____Amount spent_____
          (Include all automobile related expenses, payment, repairs, gas, washing, etc.)

Other kinds of purchases note here:

_____
_____
_____
_____
_____
_____

What feelings were elicited in you as you made each purchase listed? Do you feel good when you are shopping? Are you nervous? Is buying something an act of rebellion… do you deserve it… you can have it if you want it… you cannot stop me… it is my money… it is not your money… you have to account for it… sneak spending? Do you feel pleasure and satisfaction in your purchases? Record any thoughts for the week that you have observed. Was the money spent to impress, nurture, add value, sustain? What did you want to buy but did not buy? Why? This is the beginning of understanding what is happening for us when we spend money. The feelings we have create much of our prosperity experiences. What are they? From what are we creating?

How are Your Values reflected by the money you spend?

WEEK _____   *DATE:_____*

This exercise is not to be done until **AFTER** you have finished all of the values work. You will come back to do it for the beginning weeks.

Take each category that you spend money on this week, for example groceries. If you purchased groceries three times this week for the category "groceries" add them all together to get the amount. It isn't necessary for this exercise to list each trip. The same if you bought gas and tires for your car. The category would be automobile and you would add the two together. If you are purchasing clothing for a family, you may want to have separate categories for each individual.

CATEGORY	AMOUNT	NEED—WANT	VALUE

IS THIS A TITHING COURSE?

As I began my research I recalled that I had an ally on the topic in Eric Butterworth's writings on tithing, found in his foundational book, *Spiritual Economics, Chapter 11*. If one of the most influential Unity ministers, like Eric Butterworth, had also arrived at this awareness then perhaps my quest for ***Creating Sustainable Prosperity*** was firmly grounded in Unity Principles. I did not have to completely re-invent everything I wanted to teach – thank goodness. I merely had to remind everyone of a truth that we had already really known prior to embarking on this course together.

I contacted Unity Publishing, and the following insight on tithing from Eric Butterworth is worth studying:

Chapter 11 -- A New Look at Tithing

> *A study of the subject of prosperity invariably includes the practice of tithing. In most cases, it is taught with a dogmatism that is unparalleled in the whole study of Truth. Tithers swear by the practice and speak glowingly of the benefits that have come to them. However, many persons, feeling the "pinch" of economic stringency, have great reservations about it.*

> *The tithing idea is often given mystical roots, dating biblically to the book of Genesis, where Abraham gave a tithe of all he had to Melchizedek, king of Salem, who had blessed him. Today there are whole religious denominations that require tithing of all their adherents. Many other religious groups suggest it as a helpful discipline. Building on the foundation belief that tithing is God's law, many highly persuasive arguments are set forth.*

> *At the very outset, let us establish the point that tithing is an excellent practice that we strongly recommend to anyone who is seeking to change his or her life from indigence to affluence. And in this chapter, we want to probe deeply into the practice, beyond the superficial, illogical, and materialistic way it is normally approached. Tithing is normally encouraged for all the wrong reasons. Some of the claims made and the arguments set forth make the tithing concept a gross materialization of a beautiful spiritual law.*

> *Is the practice of tithing a fundamental in this "new insight in Truth"? Is it biblical? Was it a part of Jesus' teaching? Where are the origins? And how has it evolved to contemporary times?*

> *Bible students know that the Old Testament often refers to the practice of tithing. The classic reference is Malachi 3:10 (ASV): "Bring ye the whole tithe into the storehouse, that there may be food in my house, and prove me now herewith, saith Jehovah of hosts, if I will not open you the windows of heaven, and pour you out a blessing, that there shall not be room enough to receive it." It is a beautiful statement, sheer poetry! Who could take issue with it? Of course that is no reason to do so. However, neither is there reason to not examine the practice in the time of Malachi.*

> *Under Levitical law, the tithe was a form of taxation required of the Hebrews, a portion of the produce of the earth and of their herds. It wasn't a love offering or charitable contribution at all. In a religious form of government, a theocracy, tithing has often been the method of*

creating revenues to support the government. Since God is the true ruler, it is easily rationalized that the government treasury is the storehouse of the Lord.

In early Israel, under the leadership of Moses, the new nation was formed by dividing the body into twelve tribes. One of the tribes, the tribe of Levi, was singled out to serve as the priestly class. Again, in a theocracy, the government is managed by the priests. Thus the Levites became the bureaucracy, and the system by which they were supported was the tithe. There was nothing voluntary about it. The Mosaic code was rigidly enforced, and in some cases, infractions were punishable by death. This is the biblical source from which our contemporary practice of tithing has derived.

However, the tithe did not originate there. Some form of tithing was practiced almost universally throughout all the ancient world. We find evidences of it in Babylonia, in Persia, in Egypt, in Rome, and even in China. Keep in mind that it was a tithe tax, which probably originated as a tribute laid down by a shrewd conqueror or ruler on his subjects. It may be assumed that the custom of dedicating a tenth of the spoils of war "to the gods" in time

gave rise to a religious extension of the phrase (giving the tenth to God"). It is highly likely that when Abraham gave a tithe of his flocks to Melchizedek, the king of Salem, he was actually paying a tribute to the ruler for safe passage through his land.

Not understanding all this, or possibly not wanting to see it, religious teachers and writers, wanting to cite authorities for the contemporary tithing, have pointed to all the many instances in the Old Testament where tithe is referred to. The argument that is usually used is "if a tenth was required under law in those olden times, it is certainly no less fitting that we should give it cheerfully now." Now, without judging the merits of tithing, isn't this line of reasoning somewhat illogical? Under their law, the Israelites were bound to many restrictive observances. There are references to people actually being stoned to death for nothing more than gathering wheat on the Sabbath day, for this was a clear infraction of the fourth commandment. But, we do not put people to death in modern times for playing golf on Sunday. Ah, but the times have changed, we say. But why should the rigidity of the tithing observance remain unchanged, even if it was a giving process in biblical times, which it was not?

Jesus seemed to make a career out of upgrading the laws and observances of the Old Testament into the light and needs of contemporary times. For instance, with many of the commandments, he said in essence, "You have heard it said of old, but I say unto you..." Then he gave a practical insight for living. He was no rebel intent on breaking down the rule of ecclesiastical law. He was a Jew, reared in the traditions of the synagogue. And he said, "I have come not to abolish them [the laws] but to fulfill them" (Mt. 5:17).

If you are interested, carefully examine the Ten Commandments. They would appear to be a series of restrictive laws, outlining lines of conduct by which the Israelites must live. However, wise students of practical religion will break them down to their underlying essence, where they can see them as a supportive framework for the spiritually immature. Infants may need playpens and children may need fences to keep them from straying into danger. But as people *mature, there must come a time when they put away childish things. For instance, a sign of maturity in teenagers is when they decide to come home at a "reasonable" hour because they need the rest for school the following day, not just because their parents say so and will take away their allowance if they disobey. So it is with the idea of tithing. If we can accept the early practice as a form of "mandatory contribution," then, as with the Commandments, it was intended as a trellis by which we might be strengthened in our early period of spiritual growth. But the time must come when we let go of the rigid obligation so that we can spontaneously give in love and freedom and have the satisfaction that our giving equals or even exceeds the tithe.*

The discipline of tithing has been strongly stressed by many teachers in the field of New Thought or metaphysics. In view of his constant attempt to upgrade the Mosaic laws Jesus would have much to say on the subject. Actually, Jesus is never quoted in support of tithing. The reason is obvious: he makes only two references to the practice, and in both instances, tithing is referred to as a practice of someone who is being criticized.

In one of his tirades against the Pharisees, Jesus said: "Woe to you, scribes and Pharisees, hypocrites! For you tithe mint and dill and cumin, and have neglected the weightier matters of the law....You blind guides, straining out a gnat and swallowing a camel!" (Mt. 23:23-24) This is certainly not a recommendation of tithing.

In his parable of the Pharisee and the tax collector, the Pharisee stood and prayed "'God, I thank thee that I am not like other men, extortioners, unjust, adulterers, or even like this tax collector. I fast twice a week, I give tithes of all that I get'" (Luke 18:11-12). Then Jesus said that the tax collector would be justified, not the Pharisee. Again, no tribute to the tithing practice.

This is not to infer that Jesus condemned the practice of tithing. But it is to realize that he saw the keeping of the rigid code of tithing as a ritual far less important than the "weightier matters" of consciousness. And since he did make reference to the subject, certainly if he had felt that tithing was a "must" in his high way of spiritual unfoldment, he would have stated a clear position. But he didn't do so.

It is important to note that Jesus was very specific in his teaching of the law of giving (note that we are drawing a definite distinction between the practice of tithing and the spontaneous process of giving): "Give, and it shall be given unto you; good measure, pressed down, and shaken together, and running over, shall men give into your bosom. For with the same measure that ye mete withal it shall be measured to you again" (LK. 6:38 KJV).

The Old Testament dealt with the law of giving, which is fundamentally supportive, on the basis of the practice of tithing, which was completely coercive. Tithing was something the Israelites were required to do. Jesus taught the law of consciousness, that one always has a choice, though one must live with the effects of his or her choice. You receive as you give, and if you would receive more, you can give more, but you have complete freedom.

In the Old Testament times, tithing was an enforced discipline laid down for people who did not have the spiritual development to work with divine law. It took its place alongside hundreds of laws and observances governing everything from sanitation to meditation. As training wheels on a bicycle help a youngster to learn to ride unaided, so all these laws were right and appropriate for the people of that day.

This is not to say that we may not be benefited by "training wheels" in many aspects of our sociological and spiritual development. Certainly the practice of tithing is an excellent training process. One may read dozens of testimonials of persons who have gotten themselves on the road to a giving consciousness and who have demonstrated success and prosperity through the disciplined practice of tithing.

One classic example: William Colgate. Before leaving his home in Baltimore to seek his fortune in New York, he was advised by a family friend, an old riverboat captain, "Son, whatever work you do, do it well, take the Lord into partnership, give Him a tenth of all you make, and you will never fail." Soon Colgate was a manager of a Manhattan soap firm, and a few years later he had his own business. He always set aside ten cents of each dollar for charity. On his books, his donations were labeled, "Account with the Lord." As his profits soared, he instructed the bookkeeper to increase the amount to 20 percent, and later to 30 percent.

Ultimately, he was giving 50 percent, and yet the more he gave, the more his business flourished. Among many philanthropic gestures that his tithes gave life to were the American Bible Society, of which he was one of the first directors, and Colgate University, which now bears his name. It is a classic story of American enterprise based on the prospering influence of tithing.

It is unfortunate, however, and also misleading, that tithing is presented as a divine law rather than as a training discipline by which to work toward knowledge of the law of giving. Sometimes it is said that tithing is a magic cure for all ills. But there is no magic whatever in tithing. If prosperity or healing results from tithing, it has come through the fulfilling of the law: As you give, so you receive. Bicycle riding is based on the law of balance working with the law of inertia. The training wheels have nothing to do with the laws by which the bicycle is propelled. They simply help the rider to experience the working of the law.

Why do we insist on this distinction? Tithing is not an end but a helpful means toward the end of living totally in a giving consciousness. Too often institutions "sell" the tithing practice as a way of achieving sustained support. But fundamental to this effectiveness is helping people to understand the full scope of the law of giving. Totally overlooked is the teaching responsibility to lead the person to an understanding of the process of giving way to the divine flow. Little wonder that some people refer to tithing as the "commercial of the church." a tragic derogation of a beautiful idea.

Books on the subject of tithing are often adorned with dollar signs, suggesting that tithing is an infallible way to get rich. Again, a sickening materialization of a beautiful Truth. To tithe as a kind of good investment, expecting to get back more than one gives, is not truly giving. It is a kind of bartering, a selfish attempt to work the law instead of letting the law work you.

This materialistic approach to tithing is widespread, and ours may well be a voice crying in the wilderness. We ask only that the tither, or the person weighing the merits of the practice, think the matter through carefully.

If people get into the tithe-your-way-to-riches-and-success consciousness, they are building their house on sand. With dollar signs in their eyes, they are more concerned with what they are giving to than what they are giving from. This need not be the case. It is a question of motivation. One needs to face up to some hard questions: Do I tithe to get things or to get a greater awareness of divine law? Do I analyze the effectiveness of my tithing on the basis of my income or my general well-being?

Let us not be misunderstood on this point: giving is a fundamental spiritual law. You cannot live without giving, as you cannot live without breathing. You inhale and you exhale, on and on constantly. It is a part of the vital process of life. But there is no rule that says you must inhale so many cubic inches of air. It depends on your lung capacity and on the requirements in terms of your level of exertion. Now, it may be that a person is not breathing correctly, so a specialist may give the person some breathing exercises which can be helpful in restoring balance. In the same sense, tithing can be an excellent program to help you become established in the giving receiving rhythm.

The principle is, as we stressed in the previous chapter, in any complications you may experience in life, the most effective road to overcoming is through giving. However, tithing is not necessarily the way to a giving consciousness. It is possible that you may neglect the consciousness of giving while you are enthralled with the "magic" of tithing. Here is an example: A person desires success and prosperity in her work. She is convinced that tithing will work its magic for her. After several months of tithing, when nothing shows signs of changing in her office, she begins to get discouraged. She feels that through tithing she has "paid her dues" so a promotion or raise in salary should come through. Yet if you analyze her job performance as her superiors do, you will immediately see that she does not give much of herself to her work, is not very effective, frequently arrives late, and talks to co-workers incessantly during the day. She feels that, by tithing, things will change for her. It could be said there is a raise in salary for her, which will become effective when she does. She tithes but she does not give. She needs to begin to think give, to become more service-oriented, to go the extra mile, to be more creative in her work. Tithing can be a way of getting into a giving consciousness, but it is not a substitute for a giving attitude.

The great need is to give way to the divine flow, and tithing can be an excellent means of achieving the giving consciousness. However, the giving must involve something more than the writing of a tithe check. Malachi referred to the whole tithe. This means all of us and not just all of our money. When Jesus criticized the Pharisees for tithing without love, he could have been implying that they tithed decimally and not spiritually.

The whole tithe would appear to be exemplified in the incident where Peter and John were accosted by a crippled beggar at the Temple. Peter said to the man, "I have no silver and gold, but I give you what I have; in the name of Jesus Christ of Nazareth, walk" (Acts 3:6). Out of this complete giving consciousness, the man was healed.

Khalil Gibran, in his classic work The Prophet, says:

You give but little when you give of your possessions.
It is when you give of yourself that you truly give….
Give as in yonder valley the myrtle breathes its fragrance into space.

"Bring the whole tithe into the storehouse" could imply a commitment to work with the law in all aspects of life. Prove me now, God is saying. Prove the law in action. This involves going the second mile in meeting obligations, turning the other cheek in relationships, and forgiving until "seventy times seven." It means diligence in keeping the high watch of positive thinking and loving reactions in overcoming the world of tribulations. In other words, life is consciousness, so it is foolhardy to suppose that the law can be fulfilled by anything less than a total and broad commitment to achieving a high-level consciousness.

Jesus gave prime emphasis on giving as the way to achieve this degree of consciousness; give, and you will receive. Get the feeling of being a channel for the flow of good. Think give, and you will receive. Think of your work as giving. Think of every relationship as an opportunity to give. Give to your children. Give to your neighbors. Give to a passerby on the street. Think give. Give way. Let!

And as a part of this commitment to the giving consciousness, give of your substance, graciously, wisely, and without thought of return. Think not of what you are giving to, for that can turn the mind to condescension or giving to be seen of men. Rather think of what you are giving from and thus feel humble in realizing that you are simply giving way to the divine flow.

Certainly, a helpful and practical plan for getting order and system into your giving commitment is the way of tithing. It makes as much sense as keeping a budget, and it can be given an appropriate recognition in the budget. However, it is wise to remind yourself that the 10 percent is simply a disciplined reminder to bring the whole tithe. The giving consciousness must continue where the tithe check leaves off.

If one is sincere in the desire to grow and ultimately to put away childish things, a good plan is to use the tithing slide rule as a means of checking up on your spontaneous giving during the year. In other words, instead of following the regular ritual or writing a tithe check, work for a commitment to give way to the divine flow on a sustained basis. Just let yourself be free, as a joyous giver with no thought of contracts or bargains or great benefits of success. Take pride in the growing maturity you demonstrate throughout the year by giving the whole tithe. And then at the end of the year, when you are engaged in an audit of your fiscal year for tax purposes, total up your giving and see how close you actually come to a 10 percent giving performance. What a tremendous feeling of fulfillment you will experience when you note that your giving exceeded a tenth!

Now it could be said you have put away childish things, for the whole tithe now means no tithe, in the sense of obligation. Now you are joyously in the flow of life, through a giving consciousness. One may emphasize getting, and having as the prime goals; in spiritual consciousness, one seeks the way of giving and being.

The crux of the statement in Malachi is "I will...open you the windows of heaven, and pour you out a blessing." This is usually quoted to indicate that if you tithe, everything in heaven and Earth will fall into your lap. But how conveniently, in this instance, it is forgotten that heaven is not "up there." Jesus clearly says that the kingdom of heaven is within you. It is not a place in space but an inner potentiality of imprisoned splendor that is released through you. Thus the windows of heaven are in you. The windows of heaven are you!

You are the windows of heaven, and you will be poured out as a blessing. And because you are in the flow of limitless substance by reason of your commitment to the whole tithe, the blessing that you become is more than sufficient to deal with any situation and to meet any and all requirements.

The emphasis is often upon the giving as returning to us from God "up there" or "out there" from the world. Let us not lose sight of the principle that God can do no more for us than God can do through us. The receiving is always a greater flow from within. It may be a flow of love or guidance or life or success-producing ideas, but the receiving is in the same stream as the giving.

The faucet is opened so that it can give, and the more it gives, the greater the flow by which to give. It may provide refreshment and the means of cleanliness for a household, but it is simply busy giving of itself. It may seem impractically idealistic to say that the purpose of giving is not to receive but to give. And yet, the moment we focus on receiving, we begin to lose the flow of giving. As Jesus said, "Do not let your left hand know what your right hand is doing" (Mt. 6:3). Otherwise, you could become like the Pharisee who sounded a bell as he gave so that everyone would know of his "great largesse." In the extreme, one might become as Eugene O'Neil says of his Marco: "He is not even a mortal soul; he is only an acquisitive instinct." Give to give yet more. This is the subtle and yet powerful meaning of the injunction: Think give!

Let's hear less of tithing and more of giving. Let us not be deluded by claims of "the magic of tithing." Tithing is not a law but a technique for fulfilling the law of giving. There is no magic in it whatever, any more than there is magic in the flow of water when the tap is turned on. There is no need for magic when one works diligently to keep in the flow of life.

Understand this is not to say one should not give a tenth or more of one's income. Tithing is a powerful technique to employ through which to achieve the discipline of spontaneous giving. Ultimately you cannot really know that you are a giver of the whole tithe until you test yourself by putting away the tithing practice for a period (even a month is a good test) and still wind up with an equivalent amount through spontaneous freewill giving. It is like a child learning to ride a bike with training wheels and then continuing to use the trainers throughout life. It is unlikely that he or she will ever know if he or she could ride steadily without them.

Of course, it is vital that you get into a giving consciousness and let your hands give way to some kind of giving flow. A disciplined program of tithing is certainly a giant step in spiritual growth. We are simply suggesting that you do not stop there. Dare to take the step beyond the tithing practice.

> *Will this mean less giving to churches and institutions? On the contrary, it should lead to a more sustained and generous outpouring, but from people who are released from the pressures and stringencies of decimal giving to the joy and affluence of true spiritual giving. In the end, worthy institutions should be more effectively supported and the givers should have increasingly a sense of fulfillment in knowing, at the end of each year, that their giving has actually achieved or exceeded the tithe. People who achieve this consciousness are truly ready to step forward into the new age.*

So, this is not a class about tithing. However, it is a class about coming into right relationship with prosperity, abundance of all kinds, and creating a right relationship with money. It is a class about discovering:

- Why, and how you feel stuck when it comes to money
- How to have "more than enough," whatever that means to you
- How to understand what myths you hold about money and what money will and will not do for you
- How to let go of any fear you have around money

SO…you can give generously in all areas of your life…AND…especially in the areas that you truly, truly, truly VALUE! Let the adventure of your life begin…and begin NOW!

An Integral Approach to:

Creating Sustainable Prosperity!

Chapter 2

Your Cultural History and Story about Money

WEEK 2:_____, date

How much cash do you have in your wallet? (To the penny)   _____

Add in any cash you had at home, or in your car, as of this date: _____

Beginning Total =   _____

Any payment received in cash this week — for what:

_____

_____

How much?   _____

Number of trips to ATM?   _____

Other sources for cash?   _____

Amount of additional cash withdrawn this week?   _____

Total Cash for Week =   _____

List of cash purchases for the week: This means every purchase, a can of soda, parking meters, gum, coffee. If you spent a penny write it down. Occasion for purchase might be: essential, non-essential... wanted, needed, bored, everyone else was...

PURCHASE	AMOUNT	OCCASION FOR PURCHASE
_____	_____	_____
_____	_____	_____
_____	_____	_____
_____	_____	_____
_____	_____	_____
_____	_____	_____
_____	_____	_____
_____	_____	_____
_____	_____	_____
_____	_____	_____
_____	_____	_____
_____	_____	_____

Total Amount Spent this Week: _____

Funds on Hand at the End of Week: _____

NON-CASH EXPENDITURES:

PURCHASE	AMOUNT	OCCASION FOR PURCHASE

Total Non-Cash Expenditures this Week: $_____

Total Cash Expenditures this Week $_____

Total Weekly Expenditure $_____

LOOKING AT THIS WEEKS EXPENDITURES

Number of trips to the grocery store:_____   Amount spent: _____

Look at the individual items purchased at the grocery store. Are there items that are personal to you and not really food related?_____ Should these items be part of your food budget?_____ Notice pre-packaged items, pre-made items, i.e. frozen dinners, pizzas, canned food you simply open and heat, time saving foods. Simply notice how much you would save if you purchased fresh ingredients and made from scratch and added your own spices, etc. Lots of money is spent on groceries that is no longer eaten but are called "groceries" nevertheless. Notice any reactions:

_____

Number of meals eaten out_____By yourself_____With others_____Amount spent_____

Entertainment_____   Self_____   Family_____Amount spent_____
            (This would include movies, books, plays, ballgames, clubs, hobbies, toys, etc.)

Personal Care _____   Self_____   Family_____Amount spent_____
            (This would include haircuts, massages, toiletry items, mani—pedi, medications, etc.)

Clothing_____Self_____   Family_____Amount spent_____
            (Notice if this was an intentionally pre-planned purchase or on an impulse. Was it needed, Wanted? Were you alone or with someone else?)

Household items_____Individual purchase_____Family purchase_____Amount spent_____
(Mortgage, rent, insurance, major purchase, knick-knacks, cleaning supplies or contracted services, etc.)

Automobile Related_____Individual Car_____Family Member_____Amount spent_____
            (Include all automobile related expenses, payment, repairs, gas, washing, etc.)

Other kinds of purchases note here:

_____
_____
_____
_____
_____
_____

What feelings were elicited in you as you made each purchase listed? Do you feel good when you are shopping? Are you nervous? Is buying something an act of rebellion... do you deserve it... you can have it if you want it... you cannot stop me... it is my money... it is not your money... you have to account for it... sneak spending? Do you feel pleasure and satisfaction in your purchases? Record any thoughts for the week that you have observed. What did you want to buy but did not buy? Why? This is the beginning of understanding what is happening for us when we spend money. The feelings we have create much of our prosperity experiences. What are they? From what are we creating?

How are Your Values reflected by the money you spend?

WEEK _____   *DATE:*_____

This exercise is not to be done until **AFTER** you have finished all of the values work. You will come back to do it for the beginning weeks.

Take each category that you spend money on this week, for example groceries. If you purchased groceries three times this week for the category "groceries" add them all together to get the amount. It isn't necessary for this exercise to list each trip. The same if you bought gas and tires for your car. The category would be automobile and you would add the two together. If you are purchasing clothing for a family, you may want to have separate categories for each individual.

CATEGORY	AMOUNT	NEED—WANT	VALUE

YOUR MONEY STORY

This chapter is about each of us discovering our story about money, and on an even deeper level it is about the context through which our whole relationship with money is filtered.

- Do you have enough?
- More than enough?
- Never enough?
- How does talking about money make you feel?
- Are you willing to tell someone (talk about) how much you make; how much you owe?
- How do you handle money?
- How do you think about money?
- Is money constantly in the forefront of your mind?
- Do you never think about money does it never cross your mind?

It is important that you become really clear about what your beliefs about money are and what it represents in your life. As you work -- and you will **WORK** -- to understand your relationship with money. let us begin with a definition of money given by Charles Fillmore, Co-Founder of Unity, published in Unity's foundational book *Revealing Word,* in 1959, "**Money** — a medium of exchange and a measurement of value. The materialization of spiritual substance. The symbol of the idea of prosperity."[i]

As we look at the symbolism of money we can also look at Jacob Needleman's view of money as a symbol. He says,

> *We have to look at every aspect of our lives from the point of view of money and the force it conducts in the life of present day civilization. Love and hatred, eating and sleeping, safety and danger, work and rest, marriage, children, fear, loneliness, friendship, knowledge and art, health, sickness and death: the money factor is a determining element in all of these — sometimes plainly visible, sometimes blended into the whole fabric like a weaver's dye. Think of our relationship to nature, to ideas, to pleasure; think of our sense of self-identity and self-respect; think of where we live and with what things we surround ourselves; think of all our impulses to help others or serve a larger cause; think of all our psychological and biological needs; think of where we go, how we travel, with whom we associate — or just think of what you were doing yesterday, or what you will be doing tomorrow, or in an hour. The money factor is there, wrapped around or lodged inside everything. Think of what you want or what you dream of, for now, or next year, or for the rest of your life. It will take money, a certain definite amount.[ii]*

Despite our often stated indifference to money itself, there is no area of our life that is untouched by our view of money. Unity students study prosperity exactly because of how money touches every area of our life. Metaphysically we see it as an outer manifestation of our inner view and experience of ourselves, made totally visible for ourselves and everyone else to see.

As we start our journey to sustainable prosperity we are going to identify as clearly as possible in this moment, what **Our Money Story** *is*. We will begin to create our future based on our own conclusions and conscious choices, rather than continue living unconsciously from our history with money, or the context of **Our Money Story**. Since the day of our birth we have taken on the ideas of other people. As we become conscious spiritually, we have the opportunity to now choose those ideas that we want to have and those that we choose to let go of. Quoting Fillmore from his book ***Prosperity***, "Tell me what kind of thoughts you are holding about yourself and your neighbors, [family, parents, and formers] and I can tell you just what you may expect in the way of health, finances, and harmony in your home. Are you suspicious of your neighbors? You cannot love and trust in God if you hate and distrust [others]."[iii] I would amend Fillmore's statement to say, we cannot be prosperous or live an abundant life if we live unconsciously, if we live with a context of lack about money that others created for us.

If our current life is in any way less than totally prosperous and abundant we may see that we are either living in alignment with our past training or living in total reaction to our past training. Choosing "conscious awareness" or what I also like to call "spiritual adulthood" will allow us to attain the prosperous life that is our divine birthright. As Fillmore states in his book *Prosperity*, "We are learning

that thoughts are things and occupy 'space' in mind. We cannot have new or better ones in a place already crowded with old, weak, inefficient thoughts. A mental house cleaning is even more necessary than a material one, for the without is but a reflection of the within."[iv] He goes on to say, "Each must handle his own thoughts and overcome them by aligning them with the harmony and order of the divine thought. There is an infinite omnipresent wisdom within us that will deal with these thoughts and guide us in making the discrimination between the right and the wrong when we trust ourselves fully to its intelligence. The first step in getting your mind free from this giant bugaboo is to get a clear perception of your rights as a child of God."[v] An inherent right of ours is to build our consciousness around abundance and money, and thus increase our sustainable prosperity. When we experience prosperity or abundance issues it is our opportunity to look deeply into our own consciousness and awareness to see how we are creating this. It is difficult for most of us to own that our lack of money is not "someone else's fault". We often first go to our "yeah but's." Yeah but you don't understand, my mother, my father, my grandfather, my first significant other, my boss, my job, they don't appreciate me. "They" aren't paying me what I deserve. "They" never taught me the proper use of money. "They" never trusted me. "They" didn't save and the "yeah but's" go rolling on.

As we work to understand and own our own money story we can see what we have thought, by what is currently manifested in our life. We can decide whether those thoughts still work for us, and if they do not work for us then we can create a new money story. However, just as Fillmore taught Denials AND Affirmations, we can affirm our truth by owning "what is" and then affirming what we want to bring into existence.

A question that I have often been asked over the years is what is "spiritual" about money? If our desire is to live a spiritual life more closely connected to God, why should we even focus on money or material things? To reinforce Fillmore's teaching that "money is the materialization of spiritual energy," Joseph Campbell, noted mythologist and thinker, called [money] "congealed energy." It is human energy, your energy, symbolically held in a tangible form. When we look carefully at our financial state we are really looking at a concrete picture of our spiritual energy. It is often a very unpleasant picture. Money is only one form of human energy, of course. Other forms include physical energy, love, time, creativity, and spiritual power… the lessons you learn in one area affect all the others. What is truly wonderful about having, and seeing this money picture is that it clearly allows us to take concrete steps to change our picture. While it does not seem possible, changing our relationship with money is one of the very easiest ways to have a concrete "'burning bush" experience with the Universe. Once we realize that this level of change is possible, we have our very own proof that we can indeed do anything. We then begin to trust, begin to have proof that we can indeed create the life of our dreams. It is possible!

Let's stop again and think about actual money for a moment. Again, what is money? Money is a symbol and yet it is also a thing. It is a concrete object. When we think of money as a symbol in our spiritual world it is something that we can measure, it is a tangible substance that can be touched and that can actually be seen and we can see the effect of it in our physical worlds. Unlike other spiritual symbols it is much easier to work with and yet making changes in the way that we perceive it can affect our entire lives.

"You can count it, measure it, hold it in your hand, and use it to make things happen. In so many ways, this makes it easier to talk about and work with than most spiritual ideas. Given life's holographic nature, the Universe has clearly shown that the discoveries and the changes you make in this concrete area will affect your whole life."[vi]

Said yet another way, money clearly allows us to recognize a concrete picture of ourselves as we look at how we use money, spend money, and in general how we deal with our money. We can look at our experiences when we earn money, receive money; spend money, and even when and how we think about money. Going forward we want to have the very best relationship possible with money, not just because it will affect our bank account, but because our relationship with money reflects our relationships with those we love, those we are in community with, and even our relationship with those who share our planet. "When we direct energy consciously, our experience will be one of satisfaction and creativity. When we misuse energy, our experience will be one of frustration, disappointment and thwarted dreams."[vii]

"For most of us, money is central to our lives. Whether rich or poor we have a relationship with money as soon as we are old enough to count. Money provides us with security, stability, a way to take care of our families, make a contribution, and have fun."[viii] As we look at that list we can ask ourselves what we are seeing about our own life. Is there one or more of those words, "security, stability, a way we take care of our own families, make a contribution, have fun" that comes alive for you? Do you have enough money for each of them? If not, why not? Ask yourself, what don't I want to look at regarding me and my relationship with money? Are any of these phrases running through your mind?

- If I tell the truth about my money situation I will be embarrassed.
- I earn too much vs. I do not earn enough. Repeatedly we face the hard choice of telling the truth or trying to look good.
- I cannot talk about my financial situation.
- It is not safe to let others know how much money I have.
- Money is too personal to talk about.
- Money fuels or money frustrates my dreams.

Again, I invite you to remember that there are two aspects to reality, what we call *hard facts*, *scientifically provable concepts*, or *information that can be measured.* In Wilbur's language in Integral Theory, these things exist in the upper-right-hand quadrant. While the spiritual aspects of our lives, which are the quantum aspects, or metaphysical realities exist only in the upper-left-hand quadrant. The spiritual aspect is your own personal experience. **You** know that it is real, but you cannot explain it to someone else, you cannot really prove it. Then again there are the physical aspects of your life. In the case of money, it is the balance in your checking account, the numbers on your credit card statement, on your yearly income tax statement. In terms of Integral Theory, the facts of your financial life belong in the upper right-hand quadrant and the spiritual, quantum, metaphysical realities belong in the upper left. Both are "facts" of your life that influence the prosperity results that you are getting.

Maria Nemeth teaches it this way, "You and I are designed to bring elements from metaphysical reality into physical reality."[ix] We come to this border, the border between the spiritual and the physical reality most concretely around the aspects of money, actual cash. Actual cash is one aspect of our physical reality. For our purposes, we will say that objects in this realm have high density. You can see, taste, feel or smell them. They can be measured and are subject to the constraints of space and time. One law of this domain is called impermanence: things grow, die and are replaced. Those of us on spiritual paths have often been taught that this area is not important. Perhaps we have been taught that to have a goal of acquiring money, or assets is actually non-spiritual. The teachings of Jesus in **Matthew 6:25-34; Luke 12:22-32 (ASV)** "Therefore I say unto you, be not anxious for your life, what ye shall eat, or what ye shall drink; nor yet for your body, what ye shall put on. Is not the life more than the food, and the body than the raiment?" the famous lilies of the field teaching.

If we have been taught to take this teaching literally rather than metaphysically, thinking about money, talking about money, even the desire to acquire and deal with money in an open way may be very difficult for us. So, what is it like to think about physical reality versus metaphysical reality for you? "Whatever exists here [in metaphysical realty] is intangible and cannot be measured by the usual physical means. This is the home of imagination, vision and intention. These elements exist over time and are not necessarily subject to impermanence." [x] [they are eternal] We need to use both our metaphysical skills, our spiritual skills, **and** our physical skills, the hard facts of our life, in combination to create sustainable prosperity or sustainable abundance for ourselves. We also need to understand how our egos feel and think about money and all of the aspects of having money to change our current life experience of abundance.

This is some of the real work of this class. It is subtle. It is sometimes painful to look at and when we come face to face with our financial story it will be the beginning of a new way of seeing and living. It cannot be emphasized strongly enough that telling the truth [about our physical monetary assets] needs to take place with a liberal dose of compassion and forgiveness for oneself. It also needs to come with a liberal dose of compassion and forgiveness for our caregivers/ families and both past and present significant others because they too have a story about money.

Your History and Story about Money

You now have the chance to look at your own relationship with money. This may be your first foray into this uncharted territory. But doing the following exercises will provide you with a personal context for the work you will be doing and your current financial situation. It may seem odd to think of your life story or autobiography in terms of money. However, your experience with this form of energy began when you were very young and it is still affecting your life today.

As you answer the following questions you will be discovering the contexts of your money life. These contexts have affected all of your experiences with money as an adult up until this moment. These contexts are also relevant to your success with your desires, intentions and goals.

Many of the following questions have their basis in Suzie Orman's *The 9 Steps to Financial Freedom: Practical & Spiritual Steps So You Can Stop Worrying*:

What were your family's financial circumstances when you were born?

When did you first learn about money? How old were you? What were the circumstances?

What was the biggest amount of money you ever saw as a child?

What did you parents tell you about money that made you feel good? That made you feel bad?[xi]

Did your mother have to work when others didn't, or not have to work when others did?

Do you recall your mother's or father's relationship with money? Did you hear fights about money? If you did not live with one or both of them, pick people who were your primary care givers for this question.

What is the biggest amount of money you ever saw as a child? When did you see it? Why?

Did you steal—from piggy banks, your parents' wallets, the dime stone? What did you steal? Why

Did you friends have things you didn't? Or, did you feel ashamed of having far more than your friends did? Did you feel like your friends had nicer clothes than you did?

Were you ashamed to bring your friends home to your house? Did your friends' parents have more expensive cars than yours did? Did your friends go on better vacations than you?

Did you have any allowance? Did you get less of an allowance than your friends or siblings? Did you have to work for it, or was it given to you without your having to do chores? What did you do with it—spend it? Save it?

Did you get money for presents? Did someone tell you what to do with it? Did you do what they said?

What were the best presents, special treats, you recall receiving when you were a child? Did you have to be good to earn them?

Did you get money every time you went to see your grandparents? Have you ever given or received large gifts of money? If yes, how much? For what reason(s)? How did you feel about this?

Do you remember ever losing money? When was the earliest time? What happened?

When was the first time you bought something with money you had saved? Where were you? What did you buy? Was it money you earned or money someone gave you?

Now continuing to remember back to when you were three, twelve, or seventeen, and see what one money memory comes up that feels true, important, and keeps coming back that you haven't talked about, that's the one we want.

Do you remember your first paycheck? How did you earn it? How much was in it? What did you do with it?

Did you dream of one day having a particular job or career? Have you achieved this? Why or why not? Was the amount of money you could earn a factor in your choice of careers?

How do you relate to people who have more money that you? Less money? Have you ever lost a friend because you had too much/not enough money?

Have you ever accomplished an important task or project involving money? What was it? What did you do that made you successful? Or, was there a time when you tried but did not accomplish an important task or project regarding money? What was it? What did you do that made you unsuccessful?

If your relationship with money was a personal relationship, how would you describe it? Do you fear, love, hate, depend upon, feel possessive of or generous with money? Just write whatever comes to mind.

What were your expectations about money? Were there some aspects of money that are never discussed? Even though they are not discussed, you may know what they are. If you are married or in a committed relationship, does money expectations affect your relationship?

Where do you want to see yourself ten years from now regarding money? How much in savings? How much in investments? How much money do you see yourself making ten years from now?

Regarding money, for what do you want to be known? If people were to speak about you regarding you and your relationship with money, what would you want them to say?

If you were to characterize your own brand of money madness, how would you describe it?

When you are finished writing give your **Money Story** an appropriate title.

An Integral Approach to:

Creating Sustainable Prosperity!

Chapter 3

Money as Energy &

Your Non-Discretionary Spending

WEEK 3:_____, date

How much cash do you have in your wallet? (To the penny)   _____

Add in any cash you had at home, or in your car, as of this date: _____

Beginning Total =   _____

Any payment received in cash this week — for what:

_____

_____

How much?   _____

Number of trips to ATM?   _____

Other sources for cash?   _____

Amount of additional cash withdrawn this week?   _____

Total Cash for Week =   _____

List of cash purchases for the week: This means every purchase, a can of soda, parking meters, gum, coffee. If you spent a penny write it down. Occasion for purchase might be: essential, non-essential... wanted, needed, bored, everyone else was...

PURCHASE	AMOUNT	OCCASION FOR PURCHASE
_____	_____	_____
_____	_____	_____
_____	_____	_____
_____	_____	_____
_____	_____	_____
_____	_____	_____
_____	_____	_____
_____	_____	_____
_____	_____	_____
_____	_____	_____
_____	_____	_____
_____	_____	_____

Total Amount Spent this Week: _____

Funds on Hand at the End of Week: _____

NON-CASH EXPENDITURES:

PURCHASE	AMOUNT	OCCASION FOR PURCHASE
_____	_____	_____
_____	_____	_____
_____	_____	_____
_____	_____	_____
_____	_____	_____
_____	_____	_____
_____	_____	_____
_____	_____	_____
_____	_____	_____
_____	_____	_____
_____	_____	_____
_____	_____	_____
_____	_____	_____
_____	_____	_____
_____	_____	_____
_____	_____	_____
_____	_____	_____
_____	_____	_____
_____	_____	_____
_____	_____	_____
_____	_____	_____
_____	_____	_____
_____	_____	_____
_____	_____	_____
_____	_____	_____
_____	_____	_____
_____	_____	_____
_____	_____	_____

Total Non-Cash Expenditures this Week: $_____

Total Cash Expenditures this Week $_____

Total Weekly Expenditure $_____

LOOKING AT THIS WEEKS EXPENDITURES

Number of trips to the grocery store:_____   Amount spent: _____

Look at the individual items purchased at the grocery store. Are there items that are personal to you and not really food related?_____Should these items be part of your food budget?_____Notice pre-packaged items, pre-made items, i.e. frozen dinners, pizzas, canned food you simply open and heat, time saving foods. Simply notice how much you would save if you purchased fresh ingredients and made from scratch and added your own spices, etc. Lots of money is spent on groceries that is no longer eaten but are called "groceries" nevertheless. Notice any reactions:

_____

Number of meals eaten out_____By yourself_____With others_____Amount spent_____

Entertainment_____   Self_____   Family_____Amount spent_____
                    (*This would include movies, books, plays, ballgames, clubs, hobbies, toys, etc.*)

Personal Care _____   Self_____   Family_____Amount spent_____
                    (*This would include haircuts, massages, toiletry items, mani—pedi, medications, etc.*)

Clothing_____Self_____   Family_____Amount spent_____
          (*Notice if this was an intentionally pre-planned purchase or on an impulse. Was it needed, Wanted? Were you alone or with someone else?*)

Household items_____Individual purchase_____Family purchase_____Amount spent_____
(Mortgage, rent, insurance, major purchase, knick-knacks, cleaning supplies or contracted services, etc.)

Automobile Related_____Individual Car_____Family Member_____Amount spent_____
                    (Include all automobile related expenses, payment, repairs, gas, washing, etc.)

Other kinds of purchases note here:

_____
_____
_____
_____
_____
_____

What feelings were elicited in you as you made each purchase listed? Do you feel good when you are shopping? Are you nervous? Is buying something an act of rebellion... do you deserve it... you can have it if you want it... you cannot stop me... it is my money... it is not your money... you have to account for it... sneak spending? Do you feel pleasure and satisfaction in your purchases? Record any thoughts for the week that you have observed. What did you want to buy but did not buy? Why? This is the beginning of understanding what is happening for us when we spend money. The feelings we have create much of our prosperity experiences. What are they? From what are we creating?

How are Your Values reflected by the money you spend?

WEEK _____   *DATE:*_____

This exercise is not to be done until **AFTER** you have finished all of the values work. You will come back to do it for the beginning weeks.

Take each category that you spend money on this week, for example groceries. If you purchased groceries three times this week for the category "groceries" add them all together to get the amount. It isn't necessary for this exercise to list each trip. The same if you bought gas and tires for your car. The category would be automobile and you would add the two together. If you are purchasing clothing for a family, you may want to have separate categories for each individual.

CATEGORY	AMOUNT	NEED—WANT	VALUE

MONEY, CASH & NON-DISCRETIONARY SPENDING

Whether we are looking at paper money, coins, promissory notes or credit cards, money is really nothing more than energy. What we call money is really just a promise, a representation of something that we need or want in our lives. We exchange our life force, our time, the very hours and days of our life for a representation, a promise that we can then collect on and then use to purchase goods and services. Remember specifically 525,949 is the number of minutes we each have in a year. Now, there are the minutes that you spend working to earn your money. Every minute that we are working for money we are involved in the first part of the exchange. Depending on what you are paid per hour you might work 5 minutes or 15 minutes or even half an hour or an hour for a trip to Starbucks or McDonalds. Our housing expense is usually our greatest outlay of our money. Thirty years ago when I sold real estate in Erie, Pennsylvania, we were required to qualify homeowners. Their total housing expense was not supposed to exceed a quarter to a third of a family's take home income. I know that families housing expenses in the 21st century greatly exceed that percentage. But if we use a forty-hour week and a quarter of that, for example, a wage-earner exchanges ten hours of their life each week for a place to live.

Most of us would view this as a fair exchange, receiving shelter for ten hours of work. How about someone at minimum wage who is exchanging 70 or 80 percent of their work week or 32 hours of work for their place to live? Viewing money as energy allows us to look at the exchanges we make and notice if we are exchanging our life force in alignment with our values. Are we exchanging our lives for things that really matter to us? The Broadway show *Rent* gave us a clear image of time. They rounded a year to five hundred twenty-five thousand six hundred minutes (525,600) minutes. If we look at a year and multiplied it by 70 years, there are 36,792,000 minutes in your life. It is also not too difficult to figure out approximately how many minutes we each have left. Being attentive to our time is simply another way to evaluate how we choose to use the money that we have and earn.

 If we think of our monetary evolution in values as represented by Spiral Dynamics, at the very base in history, the survival level, there was no money. There was no medium of exchange. Food was shared or horded, as was fire, a cave, water, animal skins. It was a very basic existence. One simply either had or one did not have. One shared or one did not share. In the evolution of humankind as we progress up the spiral through the tribal level, the warrior level, and traditional level, a barter system eventually gave way to a monetary system that was based on precious metals, like silver and gold, a simpler method of monetary exchange than exchanging a cow for a few dozen chickens. Although that medium of exchange continued to exist in what we call the first world countries throughout the first half of the 20th century most of us use money as a medium of exchange.

An author who writes clearly on the topic is Jacob Needleman, he uses stories from antiquity to modern history that are still applicable to our modern monetary experiences: "Within this crucible of forces, there emerged many innovations in the sphere of financial exchanges — innovations which we now recognize as the origins of modern banking, including the widespread use of paper money and promissory notes representing money... with the advent of the industrial and scientific revolutions more and more [of] what we call money began to be the medium of exchange with all levels of society." Needleman says that "money serves the aim of self-knowledge... The rise of modern living coincides with the rise of capitalism." [xii]

It is my contention that spiritual life in the 21st century requires that we live in the world effectively as well as practice our spiritual life effectively. "In our time and culture, the battlefield of life is money. There are banks, checkbooks, credit cards, mortgages, salaries, [and] the IRS."[xiii] That philosophy blends perfectly in our dealing with, handling, spending, or saving money. True transcendence includes having the approach of a spiritual adult to all areas of our life. "The part of ourselves that must act and live our life in the material world needs to be embraced with the same attention that seeks contact with higher forces and ideals."[xiv] Not having enough money to pay our bills, to have a well-funded savings account, to go on vacation or in any way live our life fully is not living a spiritual life. Since I have been aware of living a spiritual life and been aware of the people who were teaching prosperity I have been struck by the disparity of what is taught and what is lived. I fully acknowledge that having abundance is more than the balances in our checking, saving, and investment accounts. However, it is not an abundant life without sufficient funds to fulfill our basic needs and desires.

Needleman asks some important questions:

- *What is real wealth? All we want or need... what is important.... what is secondary stuff — things, time, people, leisure?*
- *Difference about... [being] serious about money vs. obsessed with it... money as a god in our culture?*
- *How does money really help in bringing us not only security of a sort, but love, health, friendship, knowledge?*
- *What kinds of happiness or well-being have we **actually** received from material possessions of all kinds?"[xv]*

Acknowledging that money is not the only means of measuring abundance we must then also acknowledge that money touches most of the aspects of abundance in our lives that do not directly revolve around money.

As we work with these ideas on a regular basis we can then begin to respect the value of money as a tool in our lives. By seeing money as a tool we can then start the process of learning to use the tool properly. We know not to use a screw-driver as a hammer but how are we using our money? We can then ask ourselves what is:

> *The relationship between the quest for **money** and the quest for **meaning?** ... We [can then] look at every aspect of our lives from the point of view of money and the force it conducts in the life of present day civilization. Love and hatred, eating and sleeping, safety and danger, work and rest, marriage, children, fear, loneliness, friendship, knowledge and art, health, sickness and death: the money factor is a determining element in all of these — sometimes plainly visible, sometimes blended into the whole fabric like a weaver's dye. Think of our relationship to nature, to ideas, to pleasure; think of our sense of self-identity and self-respect; think of where we live and with what things we surround ourselves; think of all our impulses to help others or serve a larger cause; think of all our psychological and biological needs; think of where we go, how we travel, with whom we associate — or just think of what you were doing yesterday, or what you will be doing tomorrow, or in [what house you live, what neighborhood you live in]. The money factor is there, wrapped around or lodged inside everything. Think of what you want or what you dream of, for now, or next year, or for the rest of your life. It will take money, a certain definite amount.[xvi]*

Perhaps, like me, you have never valued money in itself. I have said many times over the course of my life that, "I don't care about money. I only value the things that money can buy". If I do not value the medium of exchange that procures the things that I value, it is like not valuing the minutes of my life, or any other wage earner's life that is contributing money for me to live. I ask myself now, how can I not value what can only come from an exchange of those precious minutes of lives? If I am not willing to think about, talk about, plan, or value money itself, the very substance that makes those things possible AND I want those things, I must believe in magic to procure them for myself. None of this is to make procuring money our primary aim in life. It is, however, to make money as a tool, in and of itself something that we value, that we examine and use wisely, because we do exchange our lives for it.

Be attentive to the difference between BEING PROSPEROUS...and FEELING PROSPEROUS

Many of our Unity prosperity classes emphasize the importance of feeling prosperous. Going out to expensive places, buying good clothes, eating at wonderful restaurants so that we can feel what it is like to have money. Now, I totally admit that expanding our horizons as to what is possible has a certain merit. We cannot aspire to levels of life that we have never experienced. However, I have experienced the downside of this as well and I have seen it negatively affect the lives of those beginning to practice it. Spending money on things that are not really wanted, needed, or used; simply because they make us feel prosperous, does not **sustainably** increase our prosperity.

We may feel prosperous as we dine, or as we carry our purchases in prestigious bags with us as we continue to shop. Many of us have found that the shot of adrenaline that is produced by that buying spree is soon lost, and then when the bills for our purchases arrive and we find that the initial luster of the purchase is gone. We have the things but they no longer as important to us as when we purchased them, we often find that the good feelings that the buying produce is only a fleeting experience. Perhaps like me you can feel in your body the endorphins kick in as you spend a day shopping. Each purchase adds a little incremental boost of well-being. I know that when I shop it feels like all is right in my world as I continue to buy things. For me it can be groceries, items for the home, or gifts for others. It is somehow the act of walking around in stores surrounded by lovely luxurious things and the act of buying itself that creates the sense of well-being for me. Marketing firms recognize this and gear their advertising to eliciting this craving in us that can only be satiated by purchasing **something...anything.** If you shop you will **find a deal, something on sale that** you cannot pass up. My contention is, hard as it sounds to say it... BUYING **THINGS** IS NOT TRUE PROSPERITY.

I can attest to the fact that for the majority of my life I felt no rush, no adrenaline over an increase in my savings account. I have never felt the satisfaction of saving for a major purchase, such as a car, and had that car paid for before I drove it off of the lot. I have always ultimately paid for everything but by then it was well used and perhaps even often repaired, or even junked. I have had friends and acquaintances that experienced great joy every time they added to their savings account, or money market funds. It is a joy that I am looking forward to and want to encourage in others. That adrenaline rush will not be diminished by the length of time we have those accounts. Rather it will be enhanced every time another deposit is made and seeing your balance increase rather than decrease. Please hear that I am also not teaching that you must never buy and must always save. But, consider again that money is energy and you are exchanging your life for a latte, a soda, a t-shirt, one more stuffed animal, or whatever it is you purchase so that you can feel better for a minute. How much of your life have you exchanged for that single item—that simply went almost straight into a landfill, or at best a garage sale or a thrift shop, perhaps even before you had even taken the price tags off?

Why focus on Money itself?

Since money exists in our world and has existed in some form since civilization began, it is important to recognize that money is one of our Spiritual Gifts — we can learn to see it as a tool that we use — to further OUR VALUES, OUR VISION, OUR MISSION for ourselves, and OUR WORLD. I want to emphasize again how we eat, where we live, where we go to school, our hobbies, what we do for entertainment, who we meet and are in relationship with are all related to money. As you look at your vision and your mission can you see a way to pursue them without using money? How would you do that? We no longer live off the land as hunters or gatherers. Most of us are no longer even self-sustaining farmers. We need shelter, food, transportation in most cases, and clothing. We need the raw materials to pursue our creative endeavors. Without money how would that work? How would we pay? Who would then pay for us to live that way? Saying that money is not important to the "higher aspects" of life is simply a way of being in denial without an affirmation to follow.

So, should accumulating money be an end in itself? Is that our purpose? I believe that the answer to that is also no. Knowing our purpose and living it, and fulfilling our dreams means that we need to have the money that is necessary to achieve our purpose, live our dream, live our values, money is essential. Living our purpose and earning enough to sustain ourselves while doing it is a fabulous desire. Hence even the title of the book, *Do What You Love the Money Will Follow* by Marcia Sinetar is perfect. Even in the spiritual world money is needed. We must recognize that money is simply another tool BUT it is a tool that we must have to live the life that we have come here to planet earth in the beginning of the twenty-first century to live.

To live the life that we have been born to live, we must overcome our myths about money. We must overcome our childhood contexts about money. Perhaps we must also overcome family or religious teachings that money is the root of all evil, you have to work hard to have money, only immoral, unethical, or crooked people have a lot of money or that money devours people, and promotes addictions. Or perhaps what we have to overcome is the other side of the issue, you must live in only the best neighborhoods, join the best clubs, shop only in the best shops and department stores to be happy. In solving our relationship with money we need to understand money for what it really is and what it is not. Are we poor if we do not have money? Are we rich if we do? As we actually contemplate and ask ourselves these kinds of questions rather than live unconsciously, we are beginning to choose our own contexts for money. As Needleman explains, we are then beginning to create new contexts around seeing money as our tool that we can then choose to use or not use: "In other times and places not everyone has wanted money above all else; people have desired salvation, beauty, power, strength, pleasure, property. But now and here, money — not necessarily even the things that money can buy, but money — is what everyone wants. The outward expenditure of mankind's energy now takes place in and through money."[xvii] In the twenty-first century our waking life is spent earning money. As the focus of our life it leads to the question, are you living your life or are you being lived by your life? How many hours in your life are spent earning money? Are you earning money to buy things that you do not really want or need? If any part of that rings true for you, are you interested in living life differently? Needleman suggests that "Our lives have become a hell not because money is too important to us but because in a certain sense, it is not important enough."[xviii] If we move to a place of actually valuing money as the tool that helps us live our values and fulfill our desires how we use it becomes a sacred activity.

How we manage the energy of money in our personal lives, the energy of money in our community's lives, in our national lives, and even in our international lives, is perhaps one of the most important and sacred questions that we can ever ask ourselves. What do these words bring up for you: avarice… greed…generosity… giving… taking…withholding…investing…saving? When we give no conscious thought to our attitude towards money it can unconsciously control our life rather than merely being another aspect of our life. When we control our money, when we see "[Money] as an instrument of material help between human beings — and therefore the range of human love — [we see that money] was an inspired invention. But as the modern world has discovered about all ingenious inventions it was a sword with two edges. All by itself, as *a thing*, a *substance*, it was useless. It was meant only for helping people directly to live in the material world, while at the same time recognizing their dependence, first upon God and then upon each other. This is no doubt why, when coinage was first invented, it was administered by the priestly class, as this is no doubt why, in many cases, the earliest coins bore a religious symbol on one side and a secular symbol on the other, God and Caesar."[xix]

Needleman additionally states that "Money [is] an instrument of emotional expression in our lonely society — the principal means of human expression."[xx] This is one of the reasons that I want us to look at what we are feeling when we spend our money. Even looking at when, what time of day we tend to spend money, and whether we are alone or with others, can be illuminating. When we spend money are we really feeling lonely, bored, or depressed and using purchasing things as a way to alleviate those feelings? Are we refusing to feel one of those feelings and thus spending money masking the feeling by feeding an addiction by buying something…anything? Understanding when and why we purchase things, even our food, can become a key to healing and wholeness for ourselves. It is a key that we can have control over reality rather easily, thereby setting a stage for the deeper healing that continues to lead to our awakening, to true spiritual adulthood.

"When it comes to money precision is essential. If you don't know how much money you have, you will never be in charge of your life, or that part of your life where money is necessary."[xxi] Reading that statement was a divine moment of awakening for me, one moment I was asleep to the value of money and the next I was awake unable to sleep again.

 We know that until we face the difficult truths about ourselves, our shadow selves, it is impossible to make a choice to change. Without facing those truths, we can go on thinking that anything that is difficult or wrong with our lives is someone else's fault, that we are blameless, and hence powerless to change our lives when in fact we are the only ones that really can make that change.

Perhaps we do not see that money is controlling our lives either by its presence or its absence. Getting control of our money situations could potentially be one of our greatest steps to the life we were born to live. What if, "Almost all the difficulties that we think of as human relations, problems involving love, honor, duty, could be resolved with a definite dollar figure… Think of a problem in your life that is particularly troubling. How much money, precisely, would be required to deal with the problem?" Everything from needing therapy to heal, to needing body work or massage to heal, requires money. How much would a really good vacation, or time off from work, go toward bringing you the fun, happiness, and joy that you deserve? *To know what money is for and what it is not for is to know how to live."*[xxii] [Italics & bold mine] There are situations where money really is the answer. It is sometimes just as much fantasy to think money is not the answer as it is to imagine it is.

When we think of awakening, or when we think of gaining total control and understanding of our financial life, or money, I am wondering about what, if any, resistance might come up for you? Again, the premise that I am working from is that in the process of getting really clear about the place of money in our lives, we are discovering one of the important secrets of our spiritual journey that has been hidden from us; much as the wisdom that Solomon sought was hidden from his view: "The knowledge that Solomon seeks is very 'expensive.' It can only be had through an exceptional quality of experience, an exceptional engagement in all the forces of life."[xxiii] Money is a huge force in our lives. Let's confront it, conqueror it, and use it as the spiritual gift that it has been intended for us to be.

What does it mean to be Prosperous?

As we delve into what it means to be prosperous, and as we uncover the facts about our financial lives, we get in touch with some of our deeper hidden truths. "It is far better to understand a central truth [about money] with the whole of oneself than it is to know many things only with the mind.... it is more important to feel what one knows — even if it is only one thing — than it is to know with the head alone a mass of theories and facts."[xxiv] So, we are searching for truth both with our intellect and with our ego, [upper right quadrant] but also with our hearts and our feeling nature [upper left quadrant]. By holding both truths in balance we are creating a life filled with *Sustainable Prosperity*. "The money question is so intractable to the seeker after meaning just because one can never grasp and feel its connection to the great questions of life and to the ideas that have been handed down over the centuries by men and women of vision."[xxv] Money in the twenty-first century is one of our demons. For some it is our chief weakness either because we are either obsessed with it or because we are in denial of its importance in our lives, or some strange combination of both. The battle between Solomon and Asmodeus really represents our battle between our essence and our false sense of self, through our egos. When Moses asks God, "Who shall I say that you are, [when talking to the people of Israel and later the Pharaoh]? God answers, "Tell the people of Israel I AM [—who] sent you." Therefore, even though that statement was written thousands of years ago it has not been pervasively heard or felt in society. We have not acknowledged that our "I AM", our essence, is an aspect and a facet of God. So when we are not living from our essence in all aspects of life, including our financial lives, we are living from our egos, our false sense of who we are

One of the basic spiritual maxims is that life is a paradox. For me that statement is a simplified version of Ken Wilber's "no one is ever 100 percent wrong." Being able to see both sides of an issue, to not only see each side, but also to understand how and why there is truth within each, is an understanding that contributes to the experience and sensation of paradox. Do we need to focus on our essence? Is it where all truth lies? That focus isin fact transformational. That it contributes to knowing the ultimate truth of *who we are*? Do we need to focus on how we show up practically in the world? Robert Brumet in his book *Living Originally*, uses the word" translational" to refer to the practices that improve our physical, material lives. In this book my contention is that getting our financial lives in order will be a huge step in improving our physical lives, the facts of Wilber's Upper Right Hand Quadrant. Not either or...but both and.

Needleman puts it this way: "Only a man who pursues both directions of life — inner and outer — will find his place not only in the social community, but in the cosmic universe. And ***all of this*** has been symbolized and facilitated with money, money that is an essential instrument both for organizing the social/survival life and for making ***space and time*** available for man to grow inwardly as well.... Think of money, then, as a device invented for organizing the satisfaction of mankind's outer needs — within a cultural context in which most forms of conduct served the purpose of evoking impressions of the inner self. Money, thus understood, is intrinsically a contradiction."[xxvi] I believe it is a contradiction because it serves us in the physical world as well as being an extension of our spiritual world.

An Integral Approach to:

Creating Sustainable Prosperity!

Chapter 4

Your Values

WEEK 4:_____, date

How much cash do you have in your wallet? (To the penny)   _____

Add in any cash you had at home, or in your car, as of this date: _____

Beginning Total =   _____

Any payment received in cash this week — for what:

_____

_____

How much?   _____

Number of trips to ATM?   _____

Other sources for cash?   _____

Amount of additional cash withdrawn this week?   _____

Total Cash for Week =   _____

List of cash purchases for the week: This means every purchase, a can of soda, parking meters, gum, coffee. If you spent a penny write it down. Occasion for purchase might be: essential, non-essential... wanted, needed, bored, everyone else was...

PURCHASE	AMOUNT	OCCASION FOR PURCHASE
_____	_____	_____
_____	_____	_____
_____	_____	_____
_____	_____	_____
_____	_____	_____
_____	_____	_____
_____	_____	_____
_____	_____	_____
_____	_____	_____
_____	_____	_____
_____	_____	_____
_____	_____	_____

Total Amount Spent this Week: _____

Funds on Hand at the End of Week: _____

NON-CASH EXPENDITURES:

PURCHASE	AMOUNT	OCCASION FOR PURCHASE
_____	_____	_____
_____	_____	_____
_____	_____	_____
_____	_____	_____
_____	_____	_____
_____	_____	_____
_____	_____	_____
_____	_____	_____
_____	_____	_____
_____	_____	_____
_____	_____	_____
_____	_____	_____
_____	_____	_____
_____	_____	_____
_____	_____	_____
_____	_____	_____
_____	_____	_____
_____	_____	_____
_____	_____	_____
_____	_____	_____
_____	_____	_____
_____	_____	_____
_____	_____	_____
_____	_____	_____
_____	_____	_____
_____	_____	_____
_____	_____	_____
_____	_____	_____

Total Non-Cash Expenditures this Week: $_____

Total Cash Expenditures this Week $_____

Total Weekly Expenditure $_____

LOOKING AT THIS WEEKS EXPENDITURES

Number of trips to the grocery store:_____   Amount spent: _____

Look at the individual items purchased at the grocery store. Are there items that are personal to you and not really food related?_____Should these items be part of your food budget?_____Notice pre-packaged items, pre-made items, i.e. frozen dinners, pizzas, canned food you simply open and heat, time saving foods. Simply notice how much you would save if you purchased fresh ingredients and made from scratch and added your own spices, etc. Lots of money is spent on groceries that is no longer eaten but are called "groceries" nevertheless. Notice any reactions:

_____

Number of meals eaten out_____By yourself_____With others_____Amount spent_____

Entertainment_____   Self_____   Family_____Amount spent_____
        (This would include movies, books, plays, ballgames, clubs, hobbies, toys, etc.)

Personal Care _____   Self_____   Family_____Amount spent_____
        (This would include haircuts, massages, toiletry items, mani—pedi, medications, etc.)

Clothing_____Self_____   Family_____Amount spent_____
    (Notice if this was an intentionally pre-planned purchase or on an impulse. Was it needed, Wanted? Were you alone or with someone else?)

Household items_____Individual purchase_____Family purchase_____Amount spent_____
(Mortgage, rent, insurance, major purchase, knick-knacks, cleaning supplies or contracted services, etc.)

Automobile Related_____Individual Car_____Family Member_____Amount spent_____
    (Include all automobile related expenses, payment, repairs, gas, washing, etc.)

Other kinds of purchases note here:

_____
_____
_____
_____
_____
_____

What feelings were elicited in you as you made each purchase listed? Do you feel good when you are shopping? Are you nervous? Is buying something an act of rebellion… do you deserve it… you can have it if you want it… you cannot stop me… it is my money… it is not your money… you have to account for it… sneak spending? Do you feel pleasure and satisfaction in your purchases? Record any thoughts for the week that you have observed. What did you want to buy but did not buy? Why? This is the beginning of understanding what is happening for us when we spend money. The feelings we have create much of our prosperity experiences. What are they? From what are we creating?

How are Your Values reflected by the money you spend?

WEEK _____   *DATE:_____*

Once you have completed your values for this week, go back to the previous weeks and do the values for the purchases that you made each of those weeks. Once you have decided what value a category has for you, you can just insert it. The work only has to be done once but the value should be inserted for each week. Doing this work diligently makes the work in Chapter 7 very easy. It is all cumulative.

Take each category that you spend money on this week, for example groceries. If you purchased groceries three times this week for the category "groceries" add them all together to get the amount. It isn't necessary for this exercise to list each trip. The same if you bought gas and tires for your car. The category would be automobile and you would add the two together. If you are purchasing clothing for a family, you may want to have separate categories for each individual.

CATEGORY	AMOUNT	NEED—WANT	VALUE

YOUR VALUES AND MONEY

Now we are moving to including some of the spiritual aspects of money in our practice. Many of us discover that our values have been significantly impacted by our care-givers as we were growing up. Fillmore put it this way, "The mind of man is like the net catching every kind of idea, and it is man's privilege and duty under the divine law to separate those that are good from those which are not good."[xxvii] We also may discover that while we think our lives are very different, we either are acting out our caregiver's values on a daily basis or we are living in total reaction, not choosing to recognize any of the values that we were given as worthwhile. As we mature, turning into not just physical adults, but spiritual adults we are very capable of determining which values we inherited over our lifetimes that we want to hold onto and which we choose to relegate to a minor role or perhaps let go of all together. We are together in this class, and in this work, because we value being. We are also in this class because we value nonbeing. We value both our ego and our essence. We are the guardians of these choices. While we may never do it perfectly our intention as well as our focus blessed by grace can take us significant distances in the directions we choose to go.

Another way to think of values was highlighted for me by Elizabeth Gilbert (of *Eat, Pray, Love* fame). When interviewed after the movie came out. She said that not all of us could or should go to Italy, India or Bali, but all of us could identify what we **really, really, really wanted.** She continued that without at least three really, really, reallys we would not be whole hearted or passionate about what we wanted. That concept is at play when we finally discover our top five values. The volume on our voices should change, as should the intensity in our voices when we talk about our values. If that isn't true as you discover your values perhaps you need to look again at the values list and reconsider your choices. The extreme end of this is; *what are you willing to sacrifice for your values?* Traditionally in this country we value freedom enough to die to preserve it. Now, I don't expect you to be willing to die for each of your values *and* I'm hoping you are beginning to see how important your values are to you. Since these are YOUR values they aren't necessarily peace, love and freedom...although they might be. Check in again with/for your passion(s) and discover for yourself your values really are, not what you *think* they should be, not what your family thinks that they should be, not what society tells you that they should be, but rather what they *really, really, really are*. That is why this is such a long involved chapter. In truth, these values aren't just relevant for looking at how you spend your money; they are relevant to how you spend your time, both professionally and personally. They are relevant in creating your personal vision and mission. They are relevant to how and where you live, where you choose to spend your money and who your friends are. Once you really understand what your values are they are the North Star that guides your entire life.

Once we have discovered what our values are, there is a very pesky part, we must also look at *if we are living* our values. When we aren't living our own values this creates a tension and frustration within us. This can manifest as stress in our lives or physical distress in our bodies. Anything that disrupts our energetic flow eventually shows up somewhere in our bodies and in our lives and can create dis-ease in our bodies. This potential disconnect also leads me to the subject of integrity.

A discussion of values isn't complete for me without also considering integrity. While integrity is offered as a value and you will have the option of selecting it, there is a basic level at work for all of us. How we relate to this is also another spoken or unspoken context from our past. I'm guessing that to have a different standard of integrity than our parents requires really conscious work. What are your standards of integrity? Do you "cheat" to pay less income tax than you owe? (This doesn't mean you don't take full advantage of the tax laws as they currently exist. i.e. mortgage credits, charitable donations etc.)What if someone pays you cash. Do you declare it? Do you notice times when it would be easy to simply take something, steal; do you give into that urge? Where else are you tempted to "cheat"? I have very close acquaintances who think nothing of taking in several movies once they have purchased one ticket and are already in the theater. These individuals would never steal something from a store but they think nothing of "stealing" movies. In the energetic world of money, we know what we give and we also receive. When we aren't in integrity in all ways it also manifests in our lives. I know that some of you are ready to argue with me on this. Look at all of the billionaires whose ethics leave much to be desired you might say. They have money beyond measure and yet their integrity is certainly in question by many. Occasionally someone like Bernie Madoff gets caught and pays the price. But in the realm of energy I know that each individual pays a price that may not be so obvious to us as we look in from the outside.

Looking at someone else's exterior and assuming that we know anything about their interior lives simply doesn't work. Look at all of the movie stars or famous people who are unhappy, lonesome and/or insecure while from the outside it looks like they have everything that they could want. In Unity we teach the law of cause and effect. I know beyond a shadow of a doubt that it is a principle that is always in effect. If we expect the "when" of the effect to be on our timeline we are often disappointed, but we know the "when" will happen.

Integrity has some facets that are universally held by most in our culture. We have words like scam, "an instance of the use of dishonest methods to acquire something of value "that's just a *scam* to bilk insurance companies for staged accidents." gyp, hustle, sting, swindle, double-cross, pyramid scheme, racket, rip-off, gouging, overcharging, hoax, or phony. (Merriam Webster on-line dictionary). Again, this is not about judging someone else. It is really not about judging ourselves either. It is about ***noticing***. It is our work to ***notice...be aware*** if we are totally in sync with the Universe in all ways. If we aren't, why aren't we? If we aren't experiencing real prosperity this is simply another place to look and notice if we have work to do in the area of integrity.

We have only to look at different cultures to see that there are many standards, many different cultural contexts that we may have been raised with. The point for this class is to notice those that you have been surrounded by in your life and then to discover your own and live by yours. Be sure that those you choose to live by are reflected in the values you choose for your life.

--

VALUE CLARIFICATION WORD LIST

Discerning your core values may seem like a simple exercise at first glance. You may have participated in many exercises that have had you name/choose your values in a few minutes, but as you go deeper into the process, you will find that discerning core values can be a complex and multifaceted endeavor.

What gives rise to your values is not simply a list of what you hold dear or that you have been told that "spiritual" people should have. You must also discern those elements of your life that you have taken on, or "inherited" from your culture, family of origin, significant others, and other places of influence. Much of what you unconsciously pursue is reflective of those things you feel you "should" be doing or what feels safe and familiar rather than what you are truly called to express through *your* core values.

You get so many messages about what "should be" important. The impact of society telling you what products to consume, the messages of our media-driven commercialism telling you to pursue exciting careers, exotic travel or immediate romance through finding the perfect mate on a quick-fix television show or a dating web site. Families of origin and the values of your childhood culture infuse you with all manner of thinking and perceptions about money, education, housing, politics and God, just to name a few. The impact of external forces on the development of what you have pursued (and not pursued) in life is extraordinary, yet most often goes unnoticed and is unconscious.

INSTRUCTIONS

This exercise is the most time consuming one in this program. It has been discovered that most individuals will need two weeks to do this section. If the individuals in your group have many hours to devote to homework it could be done in one week making this an eleven-week program. It is important that if you take two weeks that you meet during your regular class time to touch base and talk about the process and where you are in your work validating your own experience. You will be continuing your Spending Record work during both weeks.

It is important that you do each column individually with an energy break in between each column in order for this work to be really effective. I recommend that you have at least 5 different colored pencils, or pens. It makes it easier to see where a value came from as you continue the exercise.

1ST COLUMN—FAMILY OF ORIGIN (FOO)

- I recommend that before you begin this activity that you have at least an hour or so to work on each journey through the values list.
- There will be a total of 7 times that you will go through this list. DON'T try to do this all at one setting. You have two weeks for this assignment and it is better to do some each day to allow yourself to feel the differences in the values that you have acquired.
- For this exercise in the first column check the values you inherited either consciously or unconsciously from your family of origin. This is composed of those that were an intimate part

of your childhood including, aunts, uncles, grandparents, care-givers whoever you feel was a pivotal part of your childhood. Start by reflecting on your early childhood, teenage years. Close your eyes and allow yourself to feel like you are in your childhood home(s). Smell the smells, feel the feelings as you find yourself in that energy then go down the list and put a check next to a value that feels like that space.

- If you don't know the word, chances are it was not a value of your youth. Do this without editing or judging, simply put a check in the first column and continue down the list. Some of them you may have already shed or transformed into some other way of being or value. Check it anyway, so you become fully aware of the messages you have received over time. These messages impinge upon your consciousness. Begin now to discern them deeply and fully.
- **On this first time through you are checking in the column headed FOO for *Family of Origin*.**

At Least four hours minimum after you went through the list the first time. [*This is an arbitrary break. What is necessary is that you find a way to get out of the energy of the individuals that you were working with so that you can move into the next energy. This is true for each column*] You might go for a walk, do some physical work. Whatever allows you to create a fresh space for the next work session.

2ND COLUMN—RELIGION/ETHNIC GROUP (CHILDHOOD NEIGHBORHOOD) (REG)

- With a different color, go back to the beginning of the **REG *Religion or Ethnic Group (neighborhood)*** list.
- Look at the list with fresh eyes and in the second column check the values that you received from the cultural setting of your childhood, this may include **religious or ethnic groups, or neighborhoods you grew up immersed in.**
- I recommend that before you begin this activity that you have at least an hour or so to work on this journey through the values list. Start by reflecting on your early childhood, teenage years. Close your eyes and allow yourself to feel like you are in your childhood home(s). Smell the smells, feel the feelings as you find yourself in that energy then go down the list and put a check next to a value that feels like that space. Just check them as you go down the list, without editing or judging, list them. Some of them you may have already shed or transformed into some other way of being or value. Check it anyway, so you become fully aware of the messages you have received over time. These messages impinge upon your consciousness.

3RD COLUMN—SIGNIFICANT OTHERS (SO)

- With a different color, go back to the beginning of the **SO'S *Significant Other's*** list.
- Again look at the list with fresh eyes and in the third column check the values that you received from **your spouse(s)/partner(s)/ and significant other intimate people in your life.** I recommend that before you begin this activity that you have at least an hour or so to work on this journey through the values list. Start by reflecting on your early years in each relationship You may even use different colors in the same column if you have had more than one significant relationship go through and do each one separately.

- Close your eyes and allow yourself to feel like you are in the home(s) you shared. Smell the smells, feel the feelings as you find yourself in that energy then go down the list and put a check next to a value that feels like that space. You may notice that you are checking the same boxes or very different boxes. Remembering that you may or may not still hold these values but recognizing that they have impacted your life.

4TH COLUMN—MASS MEDIA/SOCIETY'S VALUES (MM)

- With a different color, go back to the beginning of the **MM *Marketing or Mass Media impact of society, television, movies, and/or advertising*** list. Look at the list with fresh eyes and in the fourth column check the values that you received from the **media of the times that you grew up in.** This varies SIGNIFICANTLY from decade to decade.
- I recommend that before you begin this activity that you have at least an hour or so to work on this journey through the values list.
- Start by reflecting on your early childhood, teenage years, and young adult years. Close your eyes and allow yourself to feel like you are watching TV, are in a movie, are reading the magazines, books etc. of your life.
- Feel the feelings you had as you were impacted; then go down the list and put a check next to a values that feels like that space, going down the fourth column with fresh eyes and allowing yourself to feel the **impact of society, mass media, television, movies, and/or advertising** and check those values that you have unconsciously received in this manner.
- Being conscious of what has impacted our thought process is valuable when we notice how we spend …or don't spend money, life energy.
- By now you may be feeling how many influences have affected you and how they have shaped who you currently are rather than who you were born to be.
- To ready yourself for the last section take some reflection time and write in your notebook or journal about what you are feeling, how you have been impacted by others' values and how they have expected you to be.

5th COLUMN—I CHOOSE THESE VALUES (ICV)

- Turn again to the beginning of the work and in the 5th column check those values that you cherish and wish to bring with you into your current life.
- Some of them may be merely intentions at this point. **IF** you want these values in your life check them. As you check them you may find that they are ones that are already checked or they may simply be values that you have come to value and want to honor in your life.

GOOD WORK! If you are like those who have already done this work you may have found this exercise to be very emotional work. Make note of those things that have come up for you. You may have noticed that there is a lot of white space around the values. Feel free to make notes on the pages that impacted you the most. You will be asked to refer back to your values in the chapters ahead as you work with releasing, creating action items and other work that is in the pages ahead.

6TH COLUM JUST TO THE RIGHT OF THE VALUE LISTED

- As you look at these lists of values that you have checked in the fifth column, put a rating in the 6th column, to the right of the word that you have checked for **YOURSELF**, rating its value 1—10. (10 I value this very much; 1 it Is important to me...but not too important)

7TH OR LAST COLUM

- Rate the degree you feel you are currently living this value. Again this may be very emotional for you if you find that you are not living something that you feel is very important to you; indicate again with a number 1—10 to what degree you live this value. (10 I always do; 1 I rarely do).
- The opposite may prove true. You may discover that you are totally living from your values and that your life is totally on track with who you truly are.

FOO (Family of Origin Values)
REF (Religious or Ethnic Group Values)
SO's (Significant Other's Values)
MM (/Mass Media's, Society's Values)
ICV (I choose these Values for myself)

FOO	REG	SO's	MM	ICV			
___	___	___	___	___	ABUNDANCE	___	___
___	___	___	___	___	ACCEPTANCE	___	___
___	___	___	___	___	ACCOMPLISHMENT	___	___
___	___	___	___	___	ACCORD	___	___
___	___	___	___	___	ACCURACY	___	___
___	___	___	___	___	ACHIEVEMENT	___	___
___	___	___	___	___	ACKNOWLEDGEMENT	___	___
___	___	___	___	___	ACTIVENESS	___	___
___	___	___	___	___	ADAPTABILITY	___	___
___	___	___	___	___	ADEQUACY	___	___
___	___	___	___	___	ADVISABILITY	___	___
___	___	___	___	___	AFFECTION	___	___
___	___	___	___	___	AFFLUENCE	___	___
___	___	___	___	___	AGGRESSIVENESS	___	___
___	___	___	___	___	AGILITY	___	___
___	___	___	___	___	AGREEABLENESS	___	___
___	___	___	___	___	AGREEMENT	___	___
___	___	___	___	___	ALERTNESS	___	___
___	___	___	___	___	ALIGNMENT	___	___
___	___	___	___	___	AMBITION	___	___
___	___	___	___	___	AMUSEMENT	___	___
___	___	___	___	___	ANTICIPATION	___	___
___	___	___	___	___	APPLICATION	___	___
___	___	___	___	___	APPRECIATION	___	___
___	___	___	___	___	APPROACHABILITY	___	___
___	___	___	___	___	APPROPRIATENESS	___	___
___	___	___	___	___	ARTICULACY	___	___
___	___	___	___	___	ASSERTIVENESS	___	___
___	___	___	___	___	ASSURANCE	___	___
___	___	___	___	___	ATHLETICISM	___	___
___	___	___	___	___	ATTENTIVENESS	___	___
___	___	___	___	___	ATTRACTIVENESS	___	___
___	___	___	___	___	AUDACITY	___	___
___	___	___	___	___	AUTHENTICITY	___	___
___	___	___	___	___	AVAILABILITY	___	___
___	___	___	___	___	AWARENESS	___	___
___	___	___	___	___	AWE	___	___
___	___	___	___	___	BALANCE	___	___
___	___	___	___	___	BEAUTY	___	___
___	___	___	___	___	BEING THE BEST	___	___

FOO	REG	SO's	MM	ICV			
___	___	___	___	___	BELONGING	___	___
___	___	___	___	___	BENEVOLENCE	___	___
___	___	___	___	___	BLISS	___	___
___	___	___	___	___	BOLDNESS	___	___
___	___	___	___	___	BRAVERY	___	___
___	___	___	___	___	BRIGHTNESS	___	___
___	___	___	___	___	BRILLIANCE	___	___
___	___	___	___	___	BUOYANCY	___	___
___	___	___	___	___	CALMNESS	___	___
___	___	___	___	___	CAMARADERIE	___	___
___	___	___	___	___	CANDOR	___	___
___	___	___	___	___	CAPABILITY	___	___
___	___	___	___	___	CARE	___	___
___	___	___	___	___	CAREFULNESS	___	___
___	___	___	___	___	CELEBRITY	___	___
___	___	___	___	___	CERTAINTY	___	___
___	___	___	___	___	CHALLENGE	___	___
___	___	___	___	___	CHARITY	___	___
___	___	___	___	___	CHARM	___	___
___	___	___	___	___	CHASTITY	___	___
___	___	___	___	___	CHEERFULNESS	___	___
___	___	___	___	___	CLARITY	___	___
___	___	___	___	___	CLEANLINESS	___	___
___	___	___	___	___	CLEAR-MINDEDNESS	___	___
___	___	___	___	___	CLOSENESS	___	___
___	___	___	___	___	COMFORT	___	___
___	___	___	___	___	COMMITMENT	___	___
___	___	___	___	___	COMPASSION	___	___
___	___	___	___	___	COMPLETION	___	___
___	___	___	___	___	COMPLIANCE	___	___
___	___	___	___	___	COMPOSURE	___	___
___	___	___	___	___	CONCENTRATION	___	___
___	___	___	___	___	CONCERN	___	___
___	___	___	___	___	CONFIDENCE	___	___
___	___	___	___	___	CONFORMITY	___	___
___	___	___	___	___	CONGRUENCY	___	___
___	___	___	___	___	CONNECTEDNESS	___	___
___	___	___	___	___	CONSCIOUSNESS	___	___
___	___	___	___	___	CONSIDERATION	___	___
___	___	___	___	___	CONSISTENCY	___	___
___	___	___	___	___	CONSTANCY	___	___
___	___	___	___	___	CONTENTMENT	___	___
___	___	___	___	___	CONTINUITY	___	___
___	___	___	___	___	CONTRIBUTION	___	___
___	___	___	___	___	CONTROL	___	___
___	___	___	___	___	CONVICTION	___	___
___	___	___	___	___	CONVIVIALITY	___	___

FOO	REG	SO's	MM	ICV			
___	___	___	___	___	COOLNESS	___	___
___	___	___	___	___	COOPERATION	___	___
___	___	___	___	___	CORDIALITY	___	___
___	___	___	___	___	CORRECTNESS	___	___
___	___	___	___	___	COURAGE	___	___
___	___	___	___	___	COURTESY	___	___
___	___	___	___	___	CRAFTINESS	___	___
___	___	___	___	___	CREATIVITY	___	___
___	___	___	___	___	CREDIBILITY	___	___
___	___	___	___	___	CUNNING	___	___
___	___	___	___	___	CURIOSITY	___	___
___	___	___	___	___	DARING	___	___
___	___	___	___	___	DECISIVENESS	___	___
___	___	___	___	___	DECORUM	___	___
___	___	___	___	___	DEFERENCE	___	___
___	___	___	___	___	DELIGHT	___	___
___	___	___	___	___	DEPENDABILITY	___	___
___	___	___	___	___	DEPTH	___	___
___	___	___	___	___	DESIRE	___	___
___	___	___	___	___	DETACHMENT	___	___
___	___	___	___	___	DETERMINATION	___	___
___	___	___	___	___	DEVELOPMENT	___	___
___	___	___	___	___	DEVOTION	___	___
___	___	___	___	___	DEVOUTNESS	___	___
___	___	___	___	___	DEXTERITY	___	___
___	___	___	___	___	DIGNITY	___	___
___	___	___	___	___	DILIGENCE	___	___
___	___	___	___	___	DIRECTION	___	___
___	___	___	___	___	DIRECTNESS	___	___
___	___	___	___	___	DISCIPLINE	___	___
___	___	___	___	___	DISCOVERY	___	___
___	___	___	___	___	DISCRETION	___	___
___	___	___	___	___	DISCRIMINATION	___	___
___	___	___	___	___	DIVERSITY	___	___
___	___	___	___	___	DOMINANCE	___	___
___	___	___	___	___	DREAMING	___	___
___	___	___	___	___	DRIVE	___	___
___	___	___	___	___	DUTY	___	___
___	___	___	___	___	DYNAMISM	___	___
___	___	___	___	___	EAGERNESS	___	___
___	___	___	___	___	EASE	___	___
___	___	___	___	___	ECONOMY	___	___
___	___	___	___	___	ECSTASY	___	___
___	___	___	___	___	EDUCATION	___	___
___	___	___	___	___	EFFECTIVENESS	___	___
___	___	___	___	___	EFFICIENCY	___	___
___	___	___	___	___	ELATION	___	___

FOO	REG	SO's	MM	ICV			
___	___	___	___	___	ELEGANCE	___	___
___	___	___	___	___	EMPATHY	___	___
___	___	___	___	___	ENCHANTMENT	___	___
___	___	___	___	___	ENCOURAGEMENT	___	___
___	___	___	___	___	ENDURANCE	___	___
___	___	___	___	___	ENERGY	___	___
___	___	___	___	___	ENJOYMENT	___	___
___	___	___	___	___	ENTERTAINMENT	___	___
___	___	___	___	___	ENTHUSIASM	___	___
___	___	___	___	___	EXALTATION	___	___
___	___	___	___	___	EXCELLENCE	___	___
___	___	___	___	___	EXCITEMENT	___	___
___	___	___	___	___	EXHILARATION	___	___
___	___	___	___	___	EXPECTANCY	___	___
___	___	___	___	___	EXPEDIENCY	___	___
___	___	___	___	___	EXPERIENCE	___	___
___	___	___	___	___	EXPERTISE	___	___
___	___	___	___	___	EXPLORATION	___	___
___	___	___	___	___	EXPRESSIVENESS	___	___
___	___	___	___	___	EXTRAVAGANCE	___	___
___	___	___	___	___	EXTROVERSION	___	___
___	___	___	___	___	EXUBERANCE	___	___
___	___	___	___	___	FAIRNESS	___	___
___	___	___	___	___	FAITH	___	___
___	___	___	___	___	FAITHFULNESS	___	___
___	___	___	___	___	FAME	___	___
___	___	___	___	___	FAMILY	___	___
___	___	___	___	___	FASCINATION	___	___
___	___	___	___	___	FASHION	___	___
___	___	___	___	___	FAVOR	___	___
___	___	___	___	___	FEARLESSNESS	___	___
___	___	___	___	___	FELICITY	___	___
___	___	___	___	___	FEROCITY	___	___
___	___	___	___	___	FIDELITY	___	___
___	___	___	___	___	FIERCENESS	___	___
___	___	___	___	___	FINANCIAL INDEPENDENCE	___	___
___	___	___	___	___	FIRMNESS	___	___
___	___	___	___	___	FITNESS	___	___
___	___	___	___	___	FLEXIBILITY	___	___
___	___	___	___	___	FLOW	___	___
___	___	___	___	___	FLUENCY	___	___
___	___	___	___	___	FOCUS	___	___
___	___	___	___	___	FORTITUDE	___	___
___	___	___	___	___	FRANKNESS	___	___
___	___	___	___	___	FREEDOM	___	___
___	___	___	___	___	FRESHNESS	___	___
___	___	___	___	___	FRIENDLINESS	___	___

FOO	REG	SO's	MM	ICV			
___	___	___	___	___	FRUGALITY	___	___
___	___	___	___	___	FUN	___	___
___	___	___	___	___	GALLANTRY	___	___
___	___	___	___	___	GENEROSITY	___	___
___	___	___	___	___	GENTILITY	___	___
___	___	___	___	___	GIVING	___	___
___	___	___	___	___	GLORY	___	___
___	___	___	___	___	GOOD	___	___
___	___	___	___	___	GOODNESS	___	___
___	___	___	___	___	GRACE	___	___
___	___	___	___	___	GRATITUDE	___	___
___	___	___	___	___	GREGARIOUSNESS	___	___
___	___	___	___	___	GROWTH	___	___
___	___	___	___	___	GUIDANCE	___	___
___	___	___	___	___	HAPPINESS	___	___
___	___	___	___	___	HARMONY	___	___
___	___	___	___	___	HEALTH	___	___
___	___	___	___	___	HEART	___	___
___	___	___	___	___	HELPFULNESS	___	___
___	___	___	___	___	HEROISM	___	___
___	___	___	___	___	HOLINESS	___	___
___	___	___	___	___	HONESTY	___	___
___	___	___	___	___	HOPEFULNESS	___	___
___	___	___	___	___	HOSPITALITY	___	___
___	___	___	___	___	HUMILITY	___	___
___	___	___	___	___	HUMOR	___	___
___	___	___	___	___	IMAGINATION	___	___
___	___	___	___	___	IMPACT	___	___
___	___	___	___	___	IMPARTIALITY	___	___
___	___	___	___	___	INDEPENDENCE	___	___
___	___	___	___	___	INDUSTRY	___	___
___	___	___	___	___	INGENUITY	___	___
___	___	___	___	___	INQUISITIVENESS	___	___
___	___	___	___	___	INSIGHTFULNESS	___	___
___	___	___	___	___	INSPIRATION	___	___
___	___	___	___	___	INTEGRITY	___	___
___	___	___	___	___	INTELLIGENCE	___	___
___	___	___	___	___	INTENSITY	___	___
___	___	___	___	___	INTEREST	___	___
___	___	___	___	___	INTIMACY	___	___
___	___	___	___	___	INTREPIDNESS	___	___
___	___	___	___	___	INTROVERSION	___	___
___	___	___	___	___	INTUITION	___	___
___	___	___	___	___	INTUITIVENESS	___	___
___	___	___	___	___	INVENTIVENESS	___	___
___	___	___	___	___	INVESTING	___	___
___	___	___	___	___	INVOLVEMENT	___	___

FOO	REG	SO's	MM	ICV			
___	___	___	___	___	JOY		
___	___	___	___	___	JUDICIOUSNESS	___	___
___	___	___	___	___	MEDITATION/STILLNESS	___	___
___	___	___	___	___	MELLOWNESS	___	___
___	___	___	___	___	METICULOUSNESS	___	___
___	___	___	___	___	MINDFULNESS	___	___
___	___	___	___	___	MODESTY	___	___
___	___	___	___	___	MOTIVATION	___	___
___	___	___	___	___	MYSTERIOUSNESS	___	___
___	___	___	___	___	NATURALNESS	___	___
___	___	___	___	___	NEATNESS	___	___
___	___	___	___	___	NERVE	___	___
___	___	___	___	___	NOBILITY	___	___
___	___	___	___	___	OBEDIENCE	___	___
___	___	___	___	___	OPEN-MINDEDNESS	___	___
___	___	___	___	___	OPENNESS	___	___
___	___	___	___	___	OPTIMISM	___	___
___	___	___	___	___	ORDER	___	___
___	___	___	___	___	ORGANIZATION	___	___
___	___	___	___	___	ORIGINALITY	___	___
___	___	___	___	___	OUTLANDISHNESS	___	___
___	___	___	___	___	OUTRAGEOUSNESS	___	___
___	___	___	___	___	PASSION	___	___
___	___	___	___	___	PEACE	___	___
___	___	___	___	___	PEACE & TRANQUILITY	___	___
___	___	___	___	___	PERCEPTIVENESS	___	___
___	___	___	___	___	PERFECTION	___	___
___	___	___	___	___	PERKINESS	___	___
___	___	___	___	___	PERSEVERANCE	___	___
___	___	___	___	___	PERSISTENCE	___	___
___	___	___	___	___	PERSONAL POWER	___	___
___	___	___	___	___	PERSUASIVENESS	___	___
___	___	___	___	___	PHILANTHROPY	___	___
___	___	___	___	___	PIETY	___	___
___	___	___	___	___	PLANNING	___	___
___	___	___	___	___	PLAYFULNESS	___	___
___	___	___	___	___	PLEASANTNESS	___	___
___	___	___	___	___	PLEASURE	___	___
___	___	___	___	___	POISE	___	___
___	___	___	___	___	POLISH	___	___
___	___	___	___	___	POPULARITY	___	___
___	___	___	___	___	POTENCY	___	___
___	___	___	___	___	POWER	___	___
___	___	___	___	___	PRACTICALITY	___	___
___	___	___	___	___	PRAGMATISM	___	___
___	___	___	___	___	PRECISION	___	___
___	___	___	___	___	PREPAREDNESS	___	___

FOO	REG	SO's	MM	ICV			
___	___	___	___	___	PRESENCE	___	___
___	___	___	___	___	PRIVACY	___	___
___	___	___	___	___	PROACTIVITY	___	___
___	___	___	___	___	PRODUCTIVENESS	___	___
___	___	___	___	___	PROFESSIONALISM	___	___
___	___	___	___	___	PROPRIETY	___	___
___	___	___	___	___	PROSPERITY	___	___
___	___	___	___	___	PRUDENCE	___	___
___	___	___	___	___	PUNCTUALITY	___	___
___	___	___	___	___	PURITY	___	___
___	___	___	___	___	QUICKNESS	___	___
___	___	___	___	___	QUIETNESS	___	___
___	___	___	___	___	READINESS	___	___
___	___	___	___	___	REALISM	___	___
___	___	___	___	___	REASON	___	___
___	___	___	___	___	REASONABLENESS	___	___
___	___	___	___	___	RECOGNITION	___	___
___	___	___	___	___	RECREATION	___	___
___	___	___	___	___	REFINEMENT	___	___
___	___	___	___	___	REFLECTION	___	___
___	___	___	___	___	REGARD	___	___
___	___	___	___	___	REGULARITY	___	___
___	___	___	___	___	RELAXATION	___	___
___	___	___	___	___	RELIABILITY	___	___
___	___	___	___	___	RELIGIOUSNESS	___	___
___	___	___	___	___	RESILIENCE	___	___
___	___	___	___	___	RESISTANCE	___	___
___	___	___	___	___	RESOLUTION	___	___
___	___	___	___	___	RESOLVE	___	___
___	___	___	___	___	RESOURCEFULNESS	___	___
___	___	___	___	___	RESPECT	___	___
___	___	___	___	___	RESPONSIVENESS	___	___
___	___	___	___	___	REST	___	___
___	___	___	___	___	RESULTS	___	___
___	___	___	___	___	REVERENCE	___	___
___	___	___	___	___	RIGHTNESS	___	___
___	___	___	___	___	RIGOR	___	___
___	___	___	___	___	RISK TAKING	___	___
___	___	___	___	___	ROMANCE	___	___
___	___	___	___	___	SACREDNESS	___	___
___	___	___	___	___	SACRIFICE	___	___
___	___	___	___	___	SAGACITY	___	___
___	___	___	___	___	SAINTLINESS	___	___
___	___	___	___	___	SANGUINITY	___	___
___	___	___	___	___	SATISFACTION	___	___
___	___	___	___	___	SECURITY	___	___
___	___	___	___	___	SELF EXPRESSION	___	___

FOO	REG	SO's	MM	ICV			
___	___	___	___	___	SELF-CONTROL	___	___
___	___	___	___	___	SELF-RELIANCE	___	___
___	___	___	___	___	SELF-SUFFICIENCY	___	___
___	___	___	___	___	SELFLESSNESS	___	___
___	___	___	___	___	SENSITIVITY	___	___
___	___	___	___	___	SENSUALITY	___	___
___	___	___	___	___	SERENITY	___	___
___	___	___	___	___	SERVICE TO OTHERS	___	___
___	___	___	___	___	SEXUAL EXPRESSION	___	___
___	___	___	___	___	SHARING	___	___
___	___	___	___	___	SHREWDNESS	___	___
___	___	___	___	___	SIGNIFICANCE	___	___
___	___	___	___	___	SILENCE	___	___
___	___	___	___	___	SILLINESS	___	___
___	___	___	___	___	SIMPLICITY	___	___
___	___	___	___	___	SINCERITY	___	___
___	___	___	___	___	SKILLFULNESS	___	___
___	___	___	___	___	SLEEP	___	___
___	___	___	___	___	SOLIDARITY	___	___
___	___	___	___	___	SOLITUDE	___	___
___	___	___	___	___	SOUNDNESS	___	___
___	___	___	___	___	SPEED	___	___
___	___	___	___	___	SPIRIT	___	___
___	___	___	___	___	SPIRITUAL GROWTH	___	___
___	___	___	___	___	SPIRITUAL PRACTICES	___	___
___	___	___	___	___	SPIRITUALITY	___	___
___	___	___	___	___	SPONTANEITY	___	___
___	___	___	___	___	STABILITY	___	___
___	___	___	___	___	STEALTH	___	___
___	___	___	___	___	STILLNESS	___	___
___	___	___	___	___	STRENGTH	___	___
___	___	___	___	___	SUCCESS	___	___
___	___	___	___	___	SUFFICIENCY	___	___
___	___	___	___	___	SUITABILITY	___	___
___	___	___	___	___	SUPERIORITY	___	___
___	___	___	___	___	SUPPORT	___	___
___	___	___	___	___	SUPREMACY	___	___
___	___	___	___	___	SURPRISE	___	___
___	___	___	___	___	SYMPATHY	___	___
___	___	___	___	___	SYNERGY	___	___
___	___	___	___	___	TEAMWORK	___	___
___	___	___	___	___	TEMPERANCE	___	___
___	___	___	___	___	THANKFULNESS	___	___
___	___	___	___	___	THOROUGHNESS	___	___
___	___	___	___	___	THOUGHTFULNESS	___	___
___	___	___	___	___	THRIFT	___	___
___	___	___	___	___	TIDINESS	___	___

FOO	REG	SO's	MM	ICV			
___	___	___	___	___	TIME	___	___
___	___	___	___	___	TIMELINESS	___	___
___	___	___	___	___	TOLERANCE	___	___
___	___	___	___	___	TRADITIONALISM	___	___
___	___	___	___	___	TRANQUILITY	___	___
___	___	___	___	___	TRANSCENDENCE	___	___
___	___	___	___	___	TRUST	___	___
___	___	___	___	___	TRUSTWORTHINESS	___	___
___	___	___	___	___	TRUTH	___	___
___	___	___	___	___	UNDERSTANDING	___	___
___	___	___	___	___	UNFLAPPABILITY	___	___
___	___	___	___	___	UNIFORMITY	___	___
___	___	___	___	___	UNIQUENESS	___	___
___	___	___	___	___	UNITY	___	___
___	___	___	___	___	USEFULNESS	___	___
___	___	___	___	___	UTILITY	___	___
___	___	___	___	___	VALOR	___	___
___	___	___	___	___	VARIETY	___	___
___	___	___	___	___	VICTORY	___	___
___	___	___	___	___	VIGOR	___	___
___	___	___	___	___	VIRTUE	___	___
___	___	___	___	___	VISION	___	___
___	___	___	___	___	VITALITY	___	___
___	___	___	___	___	VIVACITY	___	___
___	___	___	___	___	WARMTH	___	___
___	___	___	___	___	WATCHFULNESS	___	___
___	___	___	___	___	WEALTH	___	___
___	___	___	___	___	WILLFULNESS	___	___
___	___	___	___	___	WILLINGNESS	___	___
___	___	___	___	___	WINNING	___	___
___	___	___	___	___	WISDOM	___	___
___	___	___	___	___	WITTINESS	___	___
___	___	___	___	___	WONDER	___	___
___	___	___	___	___	WORK	___	___
___	___	___	___	___	WORK ETHIC	___	___
___	___	___	___	___	YOUTHFULNESS	___	___
___	___	___	___	___	ZEAL	___	___

"Our individuality is a gift given to us at birth, and we can honor that gift by making sure that we always stay true to the vision and values that have helped us become what we are in the present. There are so many forces in the modern world conspiring to rob us of our uniqueness that we should endeavor to remain always on guard. If we feel that we are making decisions based on outside influences, examining the motives underlying our preferences can help us regain our distinctive perspective on life. Creativity stems in part from the unusual and quirky aspects of our personalities as these elements of the self are what differentiate us from our many brothers and sisters in humanity. Your imagination will serve you well today when you express your individuality in everything you do in your personal and professional spheres."
Taurus Horoscope: The Authentic You, Daily OM

DISCERNING YOUR CORE VALUES

Your mission, the life you were born to live, and your guide to prosperity, is grounded in **YOUR Core Values**. In order to establish these, list all of the values that you rated as **10** in the 6th column to right of each value. Be sure to list them all no matter how long the list is.

_____
_____
_____
_____
_____
_____
_____
_____
_____
_____
_____
_____
_____
_____
_____
_____
_____
_____

Circle what you consider to be your top ten values. We will be returning to the values that we have given a 10 to in Chapter 5, and again we will come back to this page as we are completing Chapter 7.

(TO FILL IN AFTER CHAPTER 7)

_____

_____

_____

_____

_____

_____

Complete after you have filled in your Money Allocation exercise on pages 150 & 151. Notice the values that you have selected or assigned to each category. Now compare that to your values that you have given a number 10 to on the previous page. With a different color circle those values. Compare those with the values you circled after the values exercise. Notice if they are the same. Because how you spend your money reflects what you really value...if not perhaps you need to consider either your values or your spending habits. As you do this work you will be able to list with confidence your real top values because your spending and your values will match.

These are the values that you will begin with as you work to assign a value to each category that you spend money on. One category that most of us share and that most of us spend the most money on is housing costs. Discern which of your top values is represented by this category. Now, before you say that none of your top values is relevant to housing, and you HAVE to spend money on housing, I would refer you to Rev. Martha Creek whom many of you know. Martha's housing expense is very minimal. She has a room and a PO Box. She lives out of a suitcase and is traveling nearly every week of the year. I include her as an example because it is possible to live without furniture (which she has given away) mortgages, rent and expenses associated with housing. Housing is evidently NOT one of her top values.

If you find that one or more of your spending categories does not fit into your top values, there are two choices as I see it. Expand your top values, or look very closely at that expenditure and determine if you want to continue to spend your precious life energy and money in that way.

MONEY AND YOUR VALUES

Discovering what you really value is one of the most important pieces of your journey toward sustainable prosperity. The work that you have done that discovers what those values really are, as opposed to the things that you have **thought** you are supposed to value. This concept will be reinforced as you participate in this next part of the work. What you **really** value will be reflected in the way that you spend your life force, your energy, **your money**. Words are cheap. Where you put your money reflects what you really value. For the next three weeks, and looking backward at the last three weeks of your expenditures answer the following questions for each week. Starting with week one you will need to look at the different categories under discretionary (wants) and non-discretionary (needs)expenses and add all of the like expenditures together including your spending in all areas; **cash, credit, and checks (CCC)** and put them together under like categories. For example, your (mortgage/rent would combine with your utilities, maintenance costs, and household insurance. etc.) (auto expenses, car-payment, fuel, oil changes etc.) You will list each category, amount spent and your value it represents. Suggested categories (Auto, Charity, Clothing, Dining, Education, Entertainment, Housing, Groceries, Medical, Personal Care, Pets, Retirement, Savings, Taxes, Vacation) plus any others. Obviously the first week will be the hardest. Each week you continue this exercise the easier it will be because you will have many repeated kinds of expenditures. You can also notice if they change as you compare them to your values.

It is important for you to do this work individually. As you look at housing, or automobiles, expenses that almost all of us have. We may have totally different values assigned to these expenses. For some owning your own home or car represents freedom, for some an expression of beauty, for others it will represent security or some other totally different value. With some practice it becomes easy to assign a value to your various categories of expenses.

At the end of these six weeks of looking at what you spend and what value it represents for you, your discovery may be that you spend money on things that you do not value, while in fact your values are not reflected accurately by your spending. You may not be spending your money on what you really care about...or you may confirm your choice of values by looking at how you spend your money. There was a common measure back in the day that your checkbook [the way that you spend money] reflects **what you really value.** You now have the opportunity to discover if that is true and then make any changes to your spending that you desire to make. "What does it mean that against the forces of money, our inner values are almost always so weak and insubstantial?"[xxviii] Are we willing to continue living that way? Today I found that as I went to Starbucks for a soy caramel latte. I enjoyed my latte and yet considering my current budget I'm not sure how I will indicate the value that I received. I enjoy dinning out and being in that kind of an environment but because of time pressures I didn't stay to enjoy it. I had it to go. Remember none of this is about right or wrong. It is simply about noticing because what we observe we can make decisions about.

You will need to come back to these directions to create values for your six weeks of Spending Records.

An Integral Approach to:

Creating Sustainable Prosperity!

Chapter 5

Desire, Intention, & Thoughts

WEEK 5:_____, date

How much cash do you have in your wallet? (To the penny) _____

Add in any cash you had at home, or in your car, as of this date: _____

Beginning Total = _____

Any payment received in cash this week — for what:

_____

_____

How much? _____

Number of trips to ATM? _____

Other sources for cash? _____

Amount of additional cash withdrawn this week? _____

Total Cash for Week = _____

List of cash purchases for the week: This means every purchase, a can of soda, parking meters, gum, coffee. If you spent a penny write it down. Occasion for purchase might be: essential, non-essential… wanted, needed, bored, everyone else was…

PURCHASE	AMOUNT	OCCASION FOR PURCHASE
_____	_____	_____
_____	_____	_____
_____	_____	_____
_____	_____	_____
_____	_____	_____
_____	_____	_____
_____	_____	_____
_____	_____	_____
_____	_____	_____
_____	_____	_____
_____	_____	_____
_____	_____	_____

Total Amount Spent this Week: _____

Funds on Hand at the End of Week: _____

NON-CASH EXPENDITURES:

PURCHASE	AMOUNT	OCCASION FOR PURCHASE
_____	_____	_____
_____	_____	_____
_____	_____	_____
_____	_____	_____
_____	_____	_____
_____	_____	_____
_____	_____	_____
_____	_____	_____
_____	_____	_____
_____	_____	_____
_____	_____	_____
_____	_____	_____
_____	_____	_____
_____	_____	_____
_____	_____	_____
_____	_____	_____
_____	_____	_____
_____	_____	_____
_____	_____	_____
_____	_____	_____
_____	_____	_____
_____	_____	_____
_____	_____	_____
_____	_____	_____
_____	_____	_____
_____	_____	_____
_____	_____	_____
_____	_____	_____

Total Non-Cash Expenditures this Week: $_____

Total Cash Expenditures this Week $_____

Total Weekly Expenditure $_____

LOOKING AT THIS WEEKS EXPENDITURES

Number of trips to the grocery store:_____   Amount spent: _____

Look at the individual items purchased at the grocery store. Are there items that are personal to you and not really food related?_____Should these items be part of your food budget?_____Notice pre-packaged items, pre-made items, i.e. frozen dinners, pizzas, canned food you simply open and heat, time saving foods. Simply notice how much you would save if you purchased fresh ingredients and made from scratch and added your own spices, etc. Lots of money is spent on groceries that is no longer eaten but are called "groceries" nevertheless. Notice any reactions:

_____

Number of meals eaten out_____By yourself_____With others_____Amount spent_____

Entertainment_____   Self_____   Family_____Amount spent_____
          (*This would include movies, books, plays, ballgames, clubs, hobbies, toys, etc.*)

Personal Care _____   Self_____   Family_____Amount spent_____
          (*This would include haircuts, massages, toiletry items, mani—pedi, medications, etc.*)

Clothing_____Self_____   Family_____Amount spent_____
          (*Notice if this was an intentionally pre-planned purchase or on an impulse. Was it needed,*
          Wanted? Were you alone or with someone else?)

Household items_____Individual purchase_____Family purchase_____Amount spent_____
(Mortgage, rent, insurance, major purchase, knick-knacks, cleaning supplies or contracted services, etc.)

Automobile Related_____Individual Car_____Family Member_____Amount spent_____
          (Include all automobile related expenses, payment, repairs, gas, washing, etc.)

Other kinds of purchases note here:

_____
_____
_____
_____
_____
_____

What feelings were elicited in you as you made each purchase listed? Do you feel good when you are shopping? Are you nervous? Is buying something an act of rebellion... do you deserve it... you can have it if you want it... you cannot stop me... it is my money... it is not your money... you have to account for it... sneak spending? Do you feel pleasure and satisfaction in your purchases? Record any thoughts for the week that you have observed. What did you want to buy but did not buy? Why? This is the beginning of understanding what is happening for us when we spend money. The feelings we have create much of our prosperity experiences. What are they? From what are we creating?

How are Your Values reflected by the money you spend?

WEEK _____   *DATE:*_____

Once you have completed your values for this week, go back to the previous weeks and do the values for the purchases that you made each of those weeks. Once you have decided what value a category has for you, you can just insert it. The work only has to be done once but the value should be inserted for each week. Doing this work diligently makes the work in Chapter 7 very easy. It is all cumulative.

Take each category that you spend money on this week, for example groceries. If you purchased groceries three times this week for the category "groceries" add them all together to get the amount. It isn't necessary for this exercise to list each trip. The same if you bought gas and tires for your car. The category would be automobile and you would add the two together. If you are purchasing clothing for a family, you may want to have separate categories for each individual.

CATEGORY	AMOUNT	NEED—WANT	VALUE

DESIRE

In this chapter we will be looking at desires, wants, needs, our thoughts, and our intentions and goals. *Lessons in Truth* was not published first as a book but rather as a series of articles beginning in 1892. The articles were first published in Modern Thought, which later became Unity magazine. It became the first book that Unity ever published. In this, Unity's first book, Emilie Cady defined desire in the very best way that I have ever seen it described. I begin this chapter with an excerpt from Chapter 6 on Faith. It is her definition of desire used with permission from Unity Publishing.

"The Nazarene recognized the unchangeable truth that, in the unseen, the supply of every want awaits demand. When He said, 'Ask, and ye shall receive' (John 16:24), He was simply stating an unalterable truth. He knew that the instant we ask or desire (for asking is desire expressed) we touch a secret spring which starts on its way toward us the good that we want. He knew that there need not be any coaxing or pleading about it; that our asking is simply our complying with an unfailing law which is bound to work; there is no escape from it. Asking and receiving are the two ends of the same thing. There is a very close connection between them.

Asking springs from desire to possess some good. What is desire? Desire in the heart is always God tapping at the door of your consciousness with His infinite supply — a supply that is forever useless unless there be demand for it. 'Before they call, I will answer' (Isaiah 65:24). Before ever you are conscious of any lack, of any desire for more happiness, for fullness of joy, the great Father-Mother heart has desired them for you. It is He in you desiring them that you feel, and think it is only yourself (separate from Him) desiring them. With God the desire to give, and giving, are one and the same thing. Someone has said, 'Desire for anything is the thing itself in incipiency'; that is, the thing you desire is not only for you, but has already been started toward you out of the heart of God; and it is the first approach of the thing itself striking you that makes you desire it, or even think of it at all. The only way God has of letting us know of His infinite supply and His desire to make it ours is for Him to push gently on the divine spark living within each one of us. He wants you to be a strong, self-efficient man or woman, to have more power and dominion over all before you; so He quietly and silently pushes a little more of Himself, His desire, into the center of your being. He enlarges, so to speak, your real self, and at once you become conscious of new desire to be bigger, grander, stronger. If He had not pushed at the center of your being first, you would never have thought of new desires, but would have remained perfectly content as you were.

You think that you want better health, more love, a brighter, more cheerful home all your very own; in short, you want less evil (or no evil) and more good in your life. This is only God pushing at the inner door of your being, as if He were saying: 'My child, let Me in; I want to give you all good, that you may be more comfortable and happy.' 'Behold, my servants shall sing for joy of heart...And they shall build houses, and inhabit them' (Isaiah 65:13, 14, 21).

Remember this: Desire in the heart for anything is God's sure promise sent beforehand to indicate that it is yours already in the limitless realm of supply, and whatever you want you can have for the taking.

Taking is simply recognizing the law of supply and demand (even if you cannot see a sign of the supply any more than Elijah did when he had affirmed for rain, and not a cloud even so big as a man's hand was for a long time to be seen). Affirm your possession of the good that you desire; have faith in it, because you are working with divine law and cannot fail; do not be argued off your basic principle by anyone; and sooner will the heavens fall than that you fail to get that which you desire.

'All things whatsoever ye pray and ask for, believe that ye receive them, and ye shall have them' (Mark 11:24).

Knowing the law of abundant supply, and the truth that supply always precedes the demand, simply being the call that brings the supply into sight; knowing that all desire in the heart for any good is really God's desire in us and for us, how shall we obtain the fulfillment of our every desire, and that right speedily?

*'Delight thyself also in Jehovah; And he will give thee the desires of thy heart' (Psalms 37:4). Take right hold of God with an unwavering faith. Begin and continue to rejoice, and thank Him that you have (not **will** have) the desires of your heart, never losing sight of the fact that the desire is the thing itself in incipiency. If the good were not already yours in the invisible realm of supply, you could not, by any possibility, desire it.*

Someone asks: 'Suppose I desire my neighbor's wife, or his property; is that desire born of God? And can I see it fulfilled by affirming that it is mine?'

You do not and cannot, by any possibility, desire that which belongs to another. You do not desire your neighbor's wife. You desire the love that seems to you to be represented by your neighbor's wife. You desire something to fill your heart's craving for love. Affirm that there is for you a rightful and an overflowing supply, and claim its manifestation. It will surely come, and your so-called desire to possess your neighbor's wife will suddenly disappear.

So you do not in reality desire anything that belongs to your neighbor. You want the equivalent of that for which his possessions stand. You want your own. There is today an unlimited supply of all good provided in the unseen for every human being. No man must needs have less that another may have more. Your very own awaits you. Your understanding faith, or trust, is the power that will bring it to you.

Emerson said that the man who knows the law 'is sure that his welfare is dear to the heart of being…He believes that he cannot escape from his good.'

Knowing divine law and obeying it, we can forever rest from all anxiety, all fear, for 'Thou openest thy hand, and satisfies the desire of every living thing" (Psalms 145:16).'[xxix]

We live in this paradox – on the one hand desire comes from God and is to be honored, and then on the other hand it leads to a 21st century mass consumerism that leads many of us to make purchases that we frequently do not need, often ending up in a landfill that can take centuries to fully return to the earth. The media suggests that it is possible to buy happiness…at least until the next new thing comes along. The keynote of spiritual adulthood is the ability to live with, accept, and wrestle with paradox. It is our spiritual work to distinguish what we really desire from the voices of society that tell us what we should want, need, or have to be happy.

My answers about what to desire or want are only mine. I am positive that they would not fit for you, just as yours will not fit for me. Know what you value. Then by listening to the desires that flow from your values it will bring you everything your heart desires. "People who are successful attend to the important questions that are before them, whether they like these questions or not. They may not want to look at them, they may be afraid of the answer, but they are willing to answer them nevertheless."[xxx] As Spiritual Beings blessed with the gift of wisdom, we have the ability to distinguish between our essential desires (God given desires) and non-essential market-driven wants. No one judging from the outside will notice the differences. **It is important to not let your wants get in the way of your desires.** However, the self-satisfaction of attaining and enjoying your essential desires will contribute not only to a lifetime of happiness, but an increased spiritual awareness of how the Universe works that will contribute to your sustainable prosperity.

I am reminded of a personal story about wanting/desire. I had always used the word "want," beginning with "I want…." Now I totally understand that to be on the receiving end of an endless list of "I want's" is a very difficult position to be in. First of all because no one can ever satisfy the "I want's" of another person, and also because to be seen as financially responsible to fulfill all of the "I wants" of another person who is always wanting something can be a terrible burden. As a much younger woman I did live constantly in the world of I want. If I would have had more skill expressing myself I would have said something like, "that is so lovely," or "I admire it so much," or "someday I would like to have something like that myself."

I would have been able to simply enjoy the beauty of the object of my "wanting", thereby totally allowing for the fact that whoever was in the range of my voice was not required to give it to me, either then or at any time in the future. In Emilie Cady's words, I was *"desir[ing] something to fill [my] heart's craving for love"*. (Definitely a "want") However, I was in a place where it seemed that "having" would make me happy, would give me access to more friends, would make me more attractive to my husband, and the list goes on and on. At the time in question my former husband had really had it with me and he said to me, "I want, I want, I want -- that's all you ever say. You know what I want? I want you to never want again."

Now, this statement made by a beleaguered husband is totally understandable. Heard by my undeserving egoic self, it was a real stab to me. I dutifully **tried** to stop "wanting" all of the time, but, without much success most of the time, **or** sometimes I rebelled against his words and "wanted" all the time.

From today's vantage point I believe that what I wanted was indeed to be loved, to be noticed, and to be appreciated. However, then I remained convinced that if I had X, Y, or Z then I would be lovable. Notice that my example fits perfectly with Emilie's example. It was seldom really the object or experience directly that I wanted; it was the love, or the beauty that I perceived it represented. Of course I did not know that at the time. It seemed like the right house, the right clothes, the right furniture, or the right club that I belonged to would make me feel acceptable. I know that you will not be surprised to know however much I got, that it was never enough and it never worked completely the way that I envisioned.

Most of my life I had a belief that those things "mattered" to someone somewhere, and that I was constantly being judged by how I dressed, how my house looked, some exterior criteria. Now that is totally consistent with the values that I was raised with and that were reflected to me by society. However, it was not true that some omnipotent being cared whether my dishes were done or whether I had a name-brand towel or a generic one from a discount store; whether my clothes were from J.C. Penney's or Saks Fifth Avenue. I know that each of us in our lives may have been judged as lacking somehow, either in our appearance, in our clothes, or in our address. At this moment I invite you to notice that judging has always been an outer reflection of our own inner judgments of ourselves. As I look back at my life I know that some of the most "popular" successful people were neither the best-dressed nor did they live in the best neighborhood. They were simply confident in themselves and who they were. As we come from our own place of power, what we truly value most in life, we will then have the things that we most desire, those things that are most important to our inner beings.

I am here to tell you right now to "NOT DESIRE," is counterintuitive to spiritual growth. To manage our lives in such a way as to not desire anything is to live in a flat, almost depressed state. We are designed to desire. Our opportunity is to understand that much of what we truly want is really our desire expressing to reach toward the Light of Spirit with both hands totally open. It is important to allow ourselves to be fully immersed in the process of "desiring, and even wanting" and yet to know that there is no material thing or experience that we can want, that will fill the void in us. That is much different than our wanting to grasp at any and all things, or experiences. It is a wonderful thing to learn that to measure our wants against our desires and then again against our values, thus allowing us to be totally fulfilled in all of our real desires.

To learn to ask the question, "What is behind this desire?" is an even better question. If it is to be acceptable by some outside standard we can then learn to look again seeing what we really want is to achieve spiritual adulthood. None of us would give a child all of the candy that they wanted, not if we really love them. To learn to say no to some of our perceived wants that are the equal of "egoic candy" is to truly learn the value of desire. Please hear again, all desire is good. However, we all have an edit button that we can learn to use effectively that will also benefit us. Use your values as a measuring stick, not a rod.

INTENTION

One of the best works on intention that I am aware of is Lynne McTaggart's *The Intention Experiment: Using Your Thoughts to Change Your Life and the World.* The list of books that has been written about the power, that we have to manifest our reality, is endless. Learning to use this powerful tool, that is a part of each of us, is often the challenge. McTaggart provides research that proves that we really can affect the entire world with our intentions. In fact, she wrote the book that enrolls each of us in holding world-wide intentions, together, that will directly affect the affairs of our world, and hence directly affect all of us in turn. Whether or not you join with Lynne's group at www.theintentionesperiment.com, or whether you simply use her work to create your own intentions, is totally up to you. Just know that the Power of Intention will work for you to fulfill or manifest your desires.

We may believe that we are focusing our thoughts, our prayers, and our affirmations on what we desire, but often, in fact, we are being challenged to say with a clear voice, with conviction and power, what specifically, it is that we desire. Most of us find that it is even more difficult to be consistent in those thoughts from hour to hour, let alone day to day, week to week, or year to year. Often it is the case that we ask for one thing while our mind energy (deep desire) is devoted to exactly the opposite. How can this be? We may say that we want to be in a relationship with our words while we are still emotionally attached to our previous relationships, evidenced by our energetic force. Or, we may value freedom more than we value a relationship at that given moment. So, while we are occasionally saying one thing (possibly daily) with our words, the energy with which we live all of the moments of our lives we may be expressing the direct opposite (which is our deeper desire), which will, consequently, be concretely manifesting itself before our very eyes.

Sometimes this is because of the conflicted values of our lives; look at your Family of Origin values again. Now look at the values of the relationships you have been a part of and then look at your own top values. Do you see conflicts there? This can be a significant part of what really occurs when we are trying to manifest what we really want. By bringing this additional clarity to bear when we are creating intentions and becoming clear about what we want can bring new focus to our desires. When our energy is asking for one thing and our words are asking for something totally different it becomes "mush" in terms of our thoughts and desires. Then the Universe has little choice but to give us what we have asked for… more mush.

While I am fully aware that getting to the point of being clear about what we desire is often a very difficult journey, sometimes we can help ourselves in that process by at least knowing what we **do not want**. Practice in small ways. Do I want this, or this? Even those of us who waffle with statements like, "I don't care, what do YOU want?" If we are totally, honest, and really clear we really know what we want, but are simply not willing to make that concrete statement to ourselves, let alone to another person, the net effect is the same. When even being clear with our friends and family is a challenge for us, we have to practice wanting. That may sound strange to our ears. Simply begin to notice, "Do I want broccoli or green beans?" Now you may be willing to eat either, but in that moment see what would taste really good to you. What do you really, really, really, want? In a restaurant we make decisions. We do not tell the server, "Bring me whatever you want me to have."

In life many of us live that way – so practice "wanting and to be flexible." Wanting/flexible… while this is an apparent spiritual paradox it is an important one and it is best distinguished by the work of Ken Keyes in his book, *Handbook to Higher Consciousness.* In it he talks about the differences between "addiction and preference". Where we get into trouble in our lives is when we are "addicted" to having what we want. "I must have this or else." Instead, Ken is saying that we need to be really clear with ourselves and with the Universe what we want. It is also important that we simply make this a preference. "I prefer broccoli …" Spiritual adulthood is about the subtleties of spiritual life, the paradoxes that we can embrace rather than trying to make the world into simplistic black and white scenarios.

Lynne confirms this practice of setting intentions by saying that the very first thing that we need is "mental coherence". As we become clear about what we really, really, really want, then we can learn to focus our thoughts AND our energy AND our feelings. When we find ways of becoming still and actually listening to our own inner direction and when we align our thoughts and feelings it becomes much easier to manifest our desires. As we become clearer McTaggart suggests that we "merge with the 'other', and that we merge with the object of our desire, so that we are able to bring it into being in our lives. Those are her words for establishing an empathetic connection with the object of your intention. Moreover, what does merge with the other really mean? *See it, feel it, be it.* In our mind's eye, we see ourselves as being it, doing it, having it already. As children we might have called that day dreaming or pretending. Dream it as you want it to be created it in your life.

She also suggests that we can best merge with the 'other' by focusing our attention on compassion as emanates from our heart centers. While "seeing it in our minds eye" we also focus with our heart center, which is our energetic heart center to the right of our physical hearts, perhaps even holding our hands lightly over that center while we bring our attention to compassion, harmony, healing, and un-conditional love, all of which are attributes of our heart center. From that space we then also see or day dream or merge with the object of our desires.

You may have a list of twenty desires. However, it is better to only focus on one [xxxi]desire or intention at a time. Perhaps during your time of prayer and meditation you choose one each day, rotating your desires or daily focusing on the one that is currently the most important. You may simply choose the one that is choosing you at that time, the one that is already foremost in your mind. While we choose to focus on one at a time, we do this knowing that grace is holding all of our desires even if they are not the center of today's meditation.

Remember to always state your intention or affirmation in the positive knowing that it has **already** happened. **I am healthy,** not please give me health or I want to be healthy. Know that your perfect health has already been achieved. Manifestation does not come from a place of lack. It comes from a place of being full and grateful for what you already have. We work with gratitude directly later in the book in Chapter 9. It takes working all of the concepts presented in this book to really create sustainable prosperity and the life that you desire.

Specific intentions seem to work best. Use your power of visualization to **see** the condition or state of your intention as you desire it to be. This includes all of your senses. How does it feel? How does it look? How does it smell? What does it taste like? What are its sounds? If you are not visual, then just **think** about what it will be like when you are experiencing your desire. Lynne also states, "Belief in the power of intention is also vital. Keep firmly fixed in your mind your desired outcome and do not allow yourself to think of failure. Dismiss any **it -- won't-happen-to-me- type of thoughts**. This is covered more fully in Chapter 6.

I would also like to state the importance of quiet in your days. I am not just talking about meditating, or sitting in the silence. I am talking about living without sound for at least some part of your day. Not media, not TV, not your smart phone, not your iPod, not your tablet, not your car radio, CD's, MP3's, or any other form of sound. The value of silence is you get to fill that silence with your thoughts, your dreams, and allow your intuition to actually have full center stage to speak to you. Give your intention and your desires your full attention. Be a good audience. Listen to yourself. You may be amazed at the wisdom that you possess.

You can actually choose to focus your thoughts on your desires and intentions, for example, as you drive to work. That is an uninterrupted time that you have to focus on you. It is a time for you to notice what is important to you and allow yourself to **see** how your life will be when your desire is fulfilled. Imagine a time when you are driving to the job of your dreams, when your investment account has reached your desired number, when you are in the relationship of your dreams. It is important to spend as much time focused on your intentions as possible. Here is a block of time that is yours alone. Another thought, for those of you that get up in the morning and turn on the TV, or your computer, whether to hear the news, the weather, or what the latest thing is that is happening in Hollywood, simply resist the urge and be in silence. If you live with others you may certainly speak with them, perhaps sharing the dreams and visions that you have, both for yourself and for your family. Talk with and listen to your children, to your significant other, and then listen to their dreams and thoughts or projects, whatever they are willing to share with you. Listening to yourself and those you love is an important aspect of manifesting each of your individual intentions and any joint intentions that you share.

Wallace Wattles in *The Science of Getting Rich* says, "The more clear and definite you make your picture, and the more you dwell upon it, bringing out all its delightful details, the stronger your desire will be; and the stronger your desire, the easier it will be to hold your mind fixed upon the picture of what you want." xxxi He also says that "Behind your clear vision must be the purpose to realize it, to bring it out in tangible form. In the mental realm, enter at once into full enjoyment of the things you want." xxxii There is no chance of creating what you desire when you do not believe that you deserve it, or that it is possible.

The last step according to Lynne is "Move aside — surrender to the power of the universe and let go of the outcome". That is similar to Keyes' distinction of preference versus addiction. The phrase that can be added to every intention is "this or something better". Although we try to be as specific as possible our souls know what our real journey is about and what it is not about. If we have not stated our desire and intention in the clearest fashion, we then trust that the Universe is manifesting our desire in the right and perfect way.

Now, I would add to these **very important** steps of surrendering, and non-attachment, the step of **action**. To manifest your desire, it is also important that you do the things that are your actions to take to make your desire, your intention, come into being. Each step as listed by Lynne is very important, and I would add the upper right quadrant requirement that it is also important to take the steps that you outline are yours to do.

Achieving our desires requires not only the upper left part of the integral quadrant, which is the quadrant of desire, visualization, and surrender, but manifestation also requires the wholeness of the upper right segment of the quadrant that requires us to take real actions in the physical world to realize our desires.

In order for us to manifest our desires and create our intentions we must diligently be aware of and monitor our thoughts. We must believe as well as practice the notion that Charles Fillmore put forth in his book Prosperity, "We live in a very sea of inexhaustible substance, ready to come into manifestation when molded by our thought. We mold omnipresent substance with our mind and make from it all the things that our mind conceives." Again, let us translate this to make it more useful. Can we, while reclining on our couches, desire, intend, and create, all the things that our mind can conceive? From our couches we can desire, we can dream, and we can intend. In fact, it may be a wonderful place for that dreaming part of the process. It is true that having a desire drop into our living rooms fully manifested may happen occasionally. However, you stand a much better chance if you are also in action doing the things that will speed the process along. Butterworth is quoted as saying "pray but move your feet."

THOUGHTS

What moves your intentions ahead even faster is the power of your thoughts. Fillmore in *Prosperity* teaches us that "All power is given unto you both in heaven and in earth through your thought." This revolutionary idea, now over a hundred years old, is much more common place today than it was when it was first postulated. The power of positive thought has become almost a cliché, and it is my experience that clichés become clichés because they are true. When a truth is bandied about in common usage it sometimes ceases to feel profound. Whether it is Henry Ford's famous quote, "Believe you can, believe you can't, either way you are right". Winston Churchill's maxim, "A pessimist sees the difficulty in every opportunity; an optimist sees the opportunity in every difficulty", Norman Vincent Peale's, "Change your thoughts and you change your world", or even perhaps the Buddha, "We are shaped by our thoughts; we become what we think." We are surrounded by the great thinkers of our world telling us this profound wisdom.

The truth of these statements is evident. The opportunity, of course, is to practice that truth. "When you know what to think and do, then you must use your will to compel yourself to think and do the right thing," said Fillmore. Putting this simple idea into practice is not always easy, but consistently doing so will have tangible results in the events and experiences that come into being in your life.

Whether it is five minutes or five hours that we spend with our meditations and affirmations, we are left with the rest of our day, and what we are creating with those thoughts, is significant and not to be taken lightly. Every thought is creative, not simply those times we set aside for prayer, meditation, or affirmation. It is possible to learn to speak in a positive way every time you speak, even when you are expressing anger, fear, frustration, or even a profound sense of lack. Now, I totally understand that you will have to develop both a new mindset and a new vocabulary to do so. The question is, how much and how quickly you wish to manifest your desires and intentions? In the Universe there is no time schedule, there is no impatience and, in truth, as long as you are alive you still have time. Therefore, the "when" of your desired manifestation is entirely up to you. Granted, generous infusions of grace do happen from time to time. It can happen in spite of your thought practices. However, Wattles also advises you to "Guard your speech. Never speak of yourself, your affairs, or of anything else in a discouraged or discouraging way. Never admit the possibility of failure, or speak in a way that infers failure as a possibility. Never speak of the times as being hard, or of business conditions as being doubtful. Times may be hard and business doubtful for those who are on the competitive plane, but they can never be so for you; you can create what you want, and you are above fear. When others are having hard times and poor business, you will find your greatest opportunities… Always speak in terms of advancement; to do otherwise is to deny your faith, and to deny your faith is to lose it. Never allow yourself to feel disappointed."[xxxii] While Wattles wrote these lines in 1910 in the midst of a recession, Fillmore wrote *Prosperity* in the midst of the Great Depression. If they could manifest in those difficult times, then today is no different.

Now, not once in Desire, Intention, or Thought has the word "goal" been used. If you are like me the word goal sends shivers both up and down your spine. However, I am sure that you can see that attaining your desire **could** be described as a goal. Maria Nemeth uses a definition that I would like to offer you as you work (play) toward your desires. She says, "A goal is a promise that you make to yourself... 'an area or object toward which play is directed in order to score.' Remember play? Play is that action you engage in with a certain spirit of exploration and excitement. A goal is something you want, not something you should or ought to have." She also says, "Success is doing what you said you would do. **Period**."xxxvi

It is important to notice the energy you have as you read the various words. Sports are a good comparison. You do not hear athletes saying that the sport is "too hard to play." Serious athletes train with consistency and great deal of prolonged effort, and then they "play" their way toward winning. Yet often I hear that spiritual work is "too hard." It is too hard to change my thoughts and my habits. As long as you think it is too hard, too difficult, then that is the very energy you are sending into the Universe. That is one of the conflicts that create "mush" in our lives. Keep in mind that "it" is possible. You are still alive, you are still filled with breath, and with possibility. Therefore, you still can!

INSTRUCTIONS FOR DESIRE SHEETS

Below, simply brainstorm a list of what you desire. Do not miss anything you think of that you might desire. Notice that I am using the word desire not want. You may "want" an ice-cream cone. However, you probably will not elevate that to a desire. You can look, of course, at what is at the base of your desire for an ice-cream cone. It reminds you of treats you received when you were a child, good times with friends, or it may be comfort food for you… There are many things that you can learn from wanting an ice-cream cone. For this exercise, however, you may want to make your list of desires a little more expansive than such common-day items.

For example, I desire good health. I desire the ability to spend more time with my family. In the past I desired a master's degree. I desire an intimate and committed relationship…. the possibilities are endless. So, brainstorm away.

Now, to start with, choose the top several things that you really desire. Begin the work on the following pages. Date the desire and begin the process of creating your affirmations and intentions, listing the actions that you will need to take, and determining exactly the cost associated with fulfilling your desire, because there usually is a cost. For example, the master's degree I earned cost me $50,000, and I still owe over $12,000. When it comes to filling in the financial costs using pencil would be good. You may not actually know all of the true costs. Either list what you estimate the cost will be or list the financial requirement you know will exist and leave it blank. Please do not leave any item off you **_know_** will have a cost. Put your desire on the top line and go from there. I would not expect that you have this many desires to start with. However, as you continue to achieve your desires and new ones form you will be able to use the additional forms.

DESIRE

*DATE*_____

_____

INTENTION/AFFIRMATION

_____

_____

REQUIRED ACTIONS

1. _____
2. _____
3. _____
4. _____
5. _____
6. _____
7. ---
8. ---
9. ---
10. ---

FINANCIAL REQUIREMENTS

1. _____
2. _____
3. _____
4. _____
5. _____
6. _____
7. _____
8. _____
9. _____
10. _____

INDICATIONS OF ACHIEVEMENT/MANIFESTATION & DATES

_____

_____

DESIRE

*DATE*_____

_____

INTENTION/AFFIRMATION

_____

_____

REQUIRED ACTIONS

1. _____
2. _____
3. _____
4. _____
5. _____
6. _____
7. ---
8. ---
9. ---
10. ---

FINANCIAL REQUIREMENTS

1. _____
2. _____
3. _____
4. _____
5. _____
6. _____
7. _____
8. _____
9. _____
10. _____

INDICATIONS OF ACHIEVEMENT/MANIFESTATION & DATES

_____

_____

DESIRE

DATE_____

_____

INTENTION/AFFIRMATION

_____
_____

REQUIRED ACTIONS

1. _____
2. _____
3. _____
4. _____
5. _____
6. _____

7. -
8. -
9. -
10. -

FINANCIAL REQUIREMENTS

1. _____
2. _____
3. _____
4. _____
5. _____
6. _____
7. _____
8. _____
9. _____
10. _____

INDICATIONS OF ACHIEVEMENT/MANIFESTATION & DATES

_____
_____

DESIRE

DATE_____

INTENTION/AFFIRMATION

REQUIRED ACTIONS

1. _____
2. _____
3. _____
4. _____
5. _____
6. _____
7. - - - - - - - - - - - - - - - - -
8. - - - - - - - - - - - - - - - - -
9. - - - - - - - - - - - - - - - - -
10. - - - - - - - - - - - - - - - - -

FINANCIAL REQUIREMENTS

1. _____
2. _____
3. _____
4. _____
5. _____
6. _____
7. _____
8. _____
9. _____
10. _____

INDICATIONS OF ACHIEVEMENT/MANIFESTATION & DATES

DESIRE

DATE_____

_____

INTENTION/AFFIRMATION

_____

_____

REQUIRED ACTIONS

1. _____
2. _____
3. _____
4. _____
5. _____
6. _____
7. _____
8. _____
9. _____
10. _____

FINANCIAL REQUIREMENTS

1. _____
2. _____
3. _____
4. _____
5. _____
6. _____
7. _____
8. _____
9. _____
10. _____

INDICATIONS OF ACHIEVEMENT/MANIFESTATION & DATES

_____

_____

DESIRE

DATE_____

_____

INTENTION/AFFIRMATION

_____

_____

REQUIRED ACTIONS

1. _____
2. _____
3. _____
4. _____
5. _____
6. _____
7. ---
8. ---
9. ---
10. ---

FINANCIAL REQUIREMENTS

1. _____
2. _____
3. _____
4. _____
5. _____
6. _____
7. _____
8. _____
9. _____
10. _____

INDICATIONS OF ACHIEVEMENT/MANIFESTATION & DATES

_____

_____

DESIRE

DATE_____

_____

INTENTION/AFFIRMATION

_____

_____

REQUIRED ACTIONS

1. _____
2. _____
3. _____
4. _____
5. _____
6. _____
7. _____
8. _____
9. _____
10. _____

FINANCIAL REQUIREMENTS

1. _____
2. _____
3. _____
4. _____
5. _____
6. _____
7. _____
8. _____
9. _____
10. _____

INDICATIONS OF ACHIEVEMENT/MANIFESTATION & DATES

_____

_____

DESIRE

*DATE*_____

_____

INTENTION/AFFIRMATION

_____

_____

REQUIRED ACTIONS

1. _____
2. _____
3. _____
4. _____
5. _____
6. _____
7. ---
8. ---
9. ---
10. ---

FINANCIAL REQUIREMENTS

1. _____
2. _____
3. _____
4. _____
5. _____
6. _____
7. _____
8. _____
9. _____
10. _____

INDICATIONS OF ACHIEVEMENT/MANIFESTATION & DATES

_____

_____

An Integral Approach to:

Creating Sustainable Prosperity!

Chapter 6

Faith through Knowing

Income Statements

WEEK 6:_____, date

How much cash do you have in your wallet? (To the penny)   _____

Add in any cash you had at home, or in your car, as of this date: _____

Beginning Total =   _____

Any payment received in cash this week — for what:

_____

_____

How much?   _____

Number of trips to ATM?   _____

Other sources for cash?   _____

Amount of additional cash withdrawn this week?   _____

Total Cash for Week =   _____

List of cash purchases for the week: This means every purchase, a can of soda, parking meters, gum, coffee. If you spent a penny write it down. Occasion for purchase might be: essential, non-essential... wanted, needed, bored, everyone else was...

PURCHASE	AMOUNT	OCCASION FOR PURCHASE
_____	_____	_____
_____	_____	_____
_____	_____	_____
_____	_____	_____
_____	_____	_____
_____	_____	_____
_____	_____	_____
_____	_____	_____
_____	_____	_____
_____	_____	_____
_____	_____	_____

Total Amount Spent this Week: _____

Funds on Hand at the End of Week: _____

NON-CASH EXPENDITURES:

PURCHASE	AMOUNT	OCCASION FOR PURCHASE
_____	_____	_____
_____	_____	_____
_____	_____	_____
_____	_____	_____
_____	_____	_____
_____	_____	_____
_____	_____	_____
_____	_____	_____
_____	_____	_____
_____	_____	_____
_____	_____	_____
_____	_____	_____
_____	_____	_____
_____	_____	_____
_____	_____	_____
_____	_____	_____
_____	_____	_____
_____	_____	_____
_____	_____	_____
_____	_____	_____
_____	_____	_____
_____	_____	_____
_____	_____	_____
_____	_____	_____
_____	_____	_____
_____	_____	_____

Total Non-Cash Expenditures this Week: $_____

Total Cash Expenditures this Week $_____

Total Weekly Expenditure $_____

LOOKING AT THIS WEEKS EXPENDITURES

Number of trips to the grocery store:_____   Amount spent: _____

Look at the individual items purchased at the grocery store. Are there items that are personal to you and not really food related?_____Should these items be part of your food budget?_____Notice pre-packaged items, pre-made items, i.e. frozen dinners, pizzas, canned food you simply open and heat, time saving foods. Simply notice how much you would save if you purchased fresh ingredients and made from scratch and added your own spices, etc. Lots of money is spent on groceries that is no longer eaten but are called "groceries" nevertheless. Notice any reactions:

_____

Number of meals eaten out_____By yourself_____With others_____Amount spent_____

Entertainment_____   Self_____   Family_____Amount spent_____
          (*This would include movies, books, plays, ballgames, clubs, hobbies, toys, etc.*)

Personal Care _____   Self_____   Family_____Amount spent_____
          (*This would include haircuts, massages, toiletry items, mani—pedi, medications, etc.*)

Clothing_____Self_____   Family_____Amount spent_____
          (*Notice if this was an intentionally pre-planned purchase or on an impulse. Was it needed,
          Wanted? Were you alone or with someone else?*)

Household items_____Individual purchase_____Family purchase_____Amount spent_____
(Mortgage, rent, insurance, major purchase, knick-knacks, cleaning supplies or contracted services, etc.)

Automobile Related_____Individual Car_____Family Member_____Amount spent_____
          (Include all automobile related expenses, payment, repairs, gas, washing, etc.)

Other kinds of purchases note here:

_____
_____
_____
_____
_____
_____

What feelings were elicited in you as you made each purchase listed? Do you feel good when you are shopping? Are you nervous? Is buying something an act of rebellion... do you deserve it... you can have it if you want it... you cannot stop me... it is my money... it is not your money... you have to account for it... sneak spending? Do you feel pleasure and satisfaction in your purchases? Record any thoughts for the week that you have observed. What did you want to buy but did not buy? Why? This is the beginning of understanding what is happening for us when we spend money. The feelings we have create much of our prosperity experiences. What are they? From what are we creating?

How are Your Values reflected by the money you spend?

WEEK _____   *DATE:*_____

Once you have completed your values for this week, go back to the previous weeks and do the values for the purchases that you made each of those weeks. Once you have decided what value a category has for you, you can just insert it. The work only has to be done once but the value should be inserted for each week. Doing this work diligently makes the work in Chapter 7 very easy. It is all cumulative.

Take each category that you spend money on this week, for example groceries. If you purchased groceries three times this week for the category "groceries" add them all together to get the amount. It isn't necessary for this exercise to list each trip. The same if you bought gas and tires for your car. The category would be automobile and you would add the two together. If you are purchasing clothing for a family, you may want to have separate categories for each individual.

CATEGORY	AMOUNT	NEED—WANT	VALUE

FAITH

You will notice instantly that we are now focusing on the upper left quadrant in Integral Theory.

I	IT
My Spiritual Experience of Abundance Spiritual Teachings About Prosperity Transcendent Inner World How "I AM" in Relation to the Experience of Money— Context and Feelings	Material and Outer World Banking, Checkbooks Salaries, Credit Cards Mortgages the IRS Facts, Time Management Budget New Worth Take Details of Money Seriously It's up to You to Use Your Gifts Seriously, You are the Owner
WE All of the Communities We are a Part of How each Community Relates to Money The Community's Unique Context around an Organization's Finances	**ITS** Your Community's Financial Details— Profit and Loss Sheets Budgets Net Worth You are the Owner of your Community Interdependence of Human Beings Taxes—What They Buy

The worksheets we have done on our Spending Records fit into the Upper Right Quadrant. That work is about the facts, what Robert Brumet calls "translation" in his book *Living Originally*. Our Values work is about the Upper Left. It is totally our own personal experience and evaluation of ourselves as is our Money Story, and Our Desires, Our Wants, and Our Needs. Except for the Financial Worksheets all of this information is about our personal experience. It is about how we live in the realm of Spirit. It is about the manifestation of true prosperity. True abundance is about the transformation of our beliefs about money and our relationship to it. While the details about our financial will indeed be a very important part of creating sustainable prosperity in your life, prosperity is not focused only on outer financial transactions but also on our inner actions. In other words, it is about changing your consciousness and about seeing the world through a different lens. All of this work takes place in the upper left quadrant.

With this chapter we move fully into the world of metaphor, of story, of example, and of metaphysics. We cannot create a scientific measure for faith, trust, or grace, but we can feel it. We can know these concepts in our inner beings, and we can experience them for ourselves.

When it comes time to tell someone else we can stumble, rely on personal anecdotal examples, and the individuals we are trying to explain ourselves to can quickly back us into a corner with their arguments about facts, figures, and measurable data. That does not make the upper left quadrant any less real or valuable. It is simply a sign that this information belongs entirely to you and your experience.

As we move completely into the upper left quadrant we remember that it is the total experience you have of yourself. It is totally about YOUR thoughts, YOUR feelings, YOUR sensations, YOUR consciousness. You are totally the expert of this quadrant. No one can really argue with you about anything that is happening here. I want to say it again: **you and only you are in control of this quadrant**. Of course, as with any experience in life, this means that you are the ONLY one who can change anything in this quadrant. It is into this area of the intangible that we open to the impact that faith has in our lives. Often we come to the concept of faith from the prospective of doubt, particularly in this predominately modern and post-modern age—when it is trendy to doubt everything and to live from a place of skepticism. To choose faith is often to walk through the world of doubt first. So, what is faith? How is faith relevant to our experience of prosperity?

Hebrews 11:1 often comes to mind first as we attempt to describe or talk about faith: "Now faith is the substance of things hoped for, the evidence of things not seen." Even two-thousand years ago the author of Hebrews realized that faith is a very intangible experience that goes beyond the physical experiences in life. Charles Fillmore in Revealing Word describes it as follows: "The perceiving power of the mind linked with the power to shape substance. Spiritual assurance; the power to do the seemingly impossible. It is a magnetic power that draws unto us our heart's desire from the invisible spiritual substance. Faith is a deep inner knowing that that which is sought is already ours for the taking."[xxxiii] The other important Bible verse that is often quoted about faith comes from Matthew 17:19-20: "Then the disciples came to Jesus privately and said, 'Why could we not cast it out?' And He said to them, 'Because of the littleness of your faith; for truly I say to you, if you have faith as a mustard seed, you shall say to this mountain, 'Move from here to there,' and it shall move; and nothing shall be impossible to you.'" I can hear you now going... yeah... and how many mountains have you moved? Here is an example of how this can work, how you can move a mountain, and maybe even attempt to measure it in a quantifiable way, for yourself, even if others may still not see it that way.

> *A small congregation in the foothills of the Great Smokey's built a new sanctuary on a piece of land willed to them by a church member. Ten days before the new church was to open, the local building   inspector informed   the minister that   the parking   lot was*

inadequate for the size of the building. Until the church doubled the size of the parking lot, they would not be able to use the new sanctuary.

Unfortunately, the church with its undersized parking lot had used every inch of their land except for the mountain against which it had been built. In order to build more parking spaces, they would have to move the mountain out of the back yard.

Undaunted, the minister announced the next Sunday morning that he would meet that evening with all members who had "mountain moving faith." They would hold a prayer session asking God to remove the mountain from the back yard and to somehow provide enough money to have it paved and painted before the scheduled opening dedication service the following week.

At the appointed time, 24 of the congregation's 300 members assembled for prayer. They prayed for nearly three hours. At ten o'clock the minister said the final "Amen". "We'll open next Sunday as scheduled," he assured everyone. "God has never let us down before, and I believe He will be faithful this time too."

The next morning, as he was working in his study, there came a loud knock at his door. When he called "come in", a rough looking construction foreman appeared, removing his hard hat as he entered. "Excuse me, Sir. I'm from Acme Construction Company over in the next county. We're building a huge new shopping mall over there and we need some fill dirt. Would you be willing to sell us a chunk of that mountain behind the church? We'll pay you for the dirt we remove and pave all the exposed area free of charge, if we can have it right away. We can't do anything else until we get the dirt in and allow it to settle properly."

The church was dedicated the next Sunday as originally planned and there were far more members with "mountain moving faith" on opening Sunday than there had been the previous week! (Source Unknown)

Even if we knew the church, its location and the name of the contractors who came and moved the mountain, there is no way that we could prove that the contractors came to that church at exactly the right time to move the mountain and pave the parking lot so that the church could open. The story, however, either resonates with you as an example of faith being justified in the modern era, prayer being answered, or it does not. It stands as a simple example of how faith can move a mountain. Faith can never belong in the upper right quadrant.

Experiment for yourself with seeing faith as visionary. If you can see something in your mind's eye, you can see it coming into being. Your part of the bargain with the Universe is to see it being so, even when there may be physical evidence to the contrary. We may say with the father in Mark 9:24 who came to Jesus for healing, "I do believe; help my unbelief." It is our doubt, our mistrust our unbelief that we need to overcome to demonstrate faith. It is in the hardest times in our lives, the times when we doubt the most that faith is most called for. Since this class is about sustainable prosperity it is the times when our income seems not to meet our physical needs that we need to know the truth, that despite the facts contained on our financial balance sheet, we need to know that we are indeed prosperous, that we live in an abundant universe, and that the money that we need will be there when we need it. Our work is to be open to the possibility that the money that we need will come to us from expected, or unexpected, sources.

Over the course of my lifetime those sources have varied from an opportunity for a second part-time job, to a generous check coming in the mail, tax refunds that I did not expect, and even a bank error in my favor. If we combine this level of mountain moving faith with our work from the upper right quadrant, of getting our financial picture under control, of living within our incomes, and working the work in this book, we will indeed be able to move mountains. The following is my definition of faith— choosing to believe the unbelievable, while knowing that the Universe will provide, despite all apparent evidence to the contrary.

TRUST

So why talk about trust after faith? Trust for me contains elements of the "how" we can get to faith. Trust seems to unfold in stages. It builds and grows based on our own personal experiences. It does not move us from the upper left to the upper right quadrant, but it does allow us to gain a portfolio of our own experience in trusting the Universe—and other people—that can allow us to have faith in the difficult times where we need faith. I am able to trust because I can look back over my lifetime and see the times when my trust in the Universe was justified. I can list example after example based on my memories and personal experiences and the experiences of those that I have worked with. Because of these examples, I can personally move from the experience of trust to having total faith in the Universe. While I can tell you the stories you have to do the work yourself to build your own trust log. We can create and then check our own "trust logs" and assure ourselves of this powerful truth. It helps to actually write down a list of times when we have personally reaped the rewards of trusting knowing that it may help us in the future.

I look at building trust in this way. I experience trust as a declaration, a promise, made with respect to the future, giving assurance that one will do, not do, give, or not give… something. Trust is an indication of what may be expected of a person or a situation. It can be demonstrated again and again and thus built over time. I trust you because you have told me you would do something at a given time, in a given way, and you have done it, perhaps many times. Hence, I have "learned" to trust you; completely, I can rely on your integrity. I have confidence in you or in an institution. Trust unfolds in stages. This is true of both individuals and the Universe: "As above, so below, as within, so without."

Trust is an interesting concept. There is the kind of trust described above that involves caring, mutual respect, etc. Then there is the kind of trust that is devoid of that type of emotion. For example, I trust the IRS to collect my taxes, I trust that the gas meter is correct, and I trust that the sun will come up tomorrow morning, whether I see it or not. When we have built a foundation of trust with an individual or an organization it is usually cumulative and synergistic — unless our trust is betrayed in some way, which may lead us into distrust. We build trust with others, or they build trust with us, by keeping our word when we give it or when it is given to us. We build trust by being consistent or trustworthy. We build trust by maintaining confidentiality, by not gossiping, and by treating all people with respect, whether or not we like them.

Keep this philosophy in mind the next time you hear or are about to repeat a rumor:

The Test of Three

In ancient Greece (469 - 399 BC), Socrates was widely lauded for his wisdom.
One day the great philosopher came upon an acquaintance, who ran up to him excitedly and said, "Socrates, do you know what I just heard about one of your students...?"
"Wait a moment," Socrates replied. "Before you tell me, I'd like you to pass a little test. It's called the Test of Three."
"Test of Three?"
"That's correct," Socrates continued. "Before you talk to me about my student let's take a moment to test what you're going to say. The first test is Truth. Have you made absolutely sure that what you are about to tell me is true?"
"No," the man replied, "actually I just heard about it."
"All right," said Socrates. "So you don't really know if it's true or not.
Now let's try the second test; the test of Goodness. Is what you are about to tell me about my student something good?"
"No, on the contrary..."
"So," Socrates continued, "you want to tell me something bad about him even though you're not certain it's true?"
The man shrugged, a little embarrassed.
Socrates continued, "You may still pass though because there is a third test; the filter of Usefulness.
Is what you want to tell me about my student going to be useful to me?"
"No, not really..."
"Well," concluded Socrates, "if what you want to tell me is neither True nor Good nor even Useful, why tell it to me at all?"
The man was defeated and ashamed and said no more.

It should be easy for you to see how being trustworthy is beneficial to your sustainable prosperity. Paying your bills on time, limiting borrowing to unavoidable necessities, and keeping your word, can each be measured in the upper-right-hand quadrant, and it builds trust, which can be the basis of faith that is necessary to create the prosperity that will fulfill many of your desires.

GRACE

The next intangible from the upper left quadrant that I believe contributes to our sustainable prosperity is grace. Sometimes grace is soft and beautiful, adding an unexplainable touch of magic and mystery to a situation in our lives. Sometimes it comes as a flash of insight that is exactly the right and perfect solution to a particular challenge. It may provide guidance that sends us off in a totally new direction. As hard as it might to believe, or even to understand, grace can also be present in the really difficult times. That form of grace is best observed in hindsight as we notice that because of the difficult situation we chose a totally different path that then gave us a totally different insight than we would have found otherwise.

Grace is a gift from the Universe that is freely given to all of us -- when we are open to receiving it, knowing that the potentiality is always present. Adyashanti, in *Falling into Grace,* describes grace in this way: "Grace is simply that which opens our hearts, that which has the capacity to come in and open our perceptions about life." As we are open to grace we realize that we do not have to struggle so hard. We do not have to fight with life. We do not have to try and control every aspect of our lives. Here is where we simply become open and receptive to the living spirit of truth. Here is where we allow, invite, and choose to be willing to receive that which comes to us…that which already is.

Applying grace to our sustainable prosperity is to do all of the work that is ours to do to get our financial affairs in order. Build a level of trust with our financial affairs and those who are a part of our lives. Have faith that the Universe is fulfilling all of our needs and allow grace to make it so for us.

KNOWING

This is the deepest, the truest aspect of faith and trust, and it is also the most difficult to talk about. One of the first things that I invite you to notice is that you can never "know" for another person, and they can never "know" for you. When another person is involved all that we can do is "think" or "assume" what is true for THEM—unless they confirm it for us. It is firmly lodged in the upper left hand of the Integral Quadrant. Like our "I am," it is closely linked with our experience of the Divine, and therefore is entirely personal. In *Revealing Word*, Charles Fillmore defines knowing this way, "There is in man a knowing capacity transcending intellectual knowledge. Nearly everyone has at some time touched this hidden wisdom and has been more or less astonished at its revelations. The knowing that man receives from the direct fusion of the Mind of God with his mind is real spiritual knowing."[xxxiv]

Knowing is moving from trust to faith, and then experiencing grace in all levels of your experience so that you can move to knowing on an unshakable cellular level that, truly, "all is well" in your financial affairs, and in your life.

I'd like to give you a simple personal example of knowing as described by my oldest daughter who graduated from Drexel University in the 80's. For those of you who aren't familiar with Philadelphia, particularly the part where Drexel is located, it is bordered on several sides by what can best be described as "bad" neighborhoods. It is about three miles from the Center City. She used to walk to the city at night, take the train or the bus back, and for a girl who grew up in the suburbs it was amazing and terrifying for me as her mother. Her oldest daughter will be a college freshman soon and we were talking about her experience in the city. She said it never even crossed her mind at any time that she wasn't safe. Even when an older African American gentleman [an angel?] said "Honey, what are you doing here"? She told him and he offered to ride with her to a different part of the neighborhood and told her she shouldn't *ever* come back to that part where he found her. She never had any problems in her four years of college...not one. I know you can hear her "MOM...I'm fine." She didn't have faith that she would be okay. She *knew* that she would be okay it didn't ever occur to her she would be... and she was. That is knowing. That is how it can manifest in us. You won't be able to explain it to anyone else and you will know

INCOME STATEMENT

I have included income in the chapter with faith and trust because you have faith that you will be paid on time for your work. You trust that the money that the government said that they would pay you will be paid on time. As evidenced by the government shutdown of October 2013, this is a matter of faith and trust. We trust our financial institutions to honor their commitments to us.

List every source of income that you have. Look at your gross income (not the amount you bring home after everything is taken out, but actually the entire amount BEFORE anything is taken out). If you have to contact your employers to get this information, then do it. It is important for you to understand exactly how much you actually earn. We will look at this on an annual basis and then we will divide it by twelve and fifty-two to look at it on a monthly and weekly basis. Also keep track of your net income as you will need it on the second worksheet. For Other Income, if you have many streams of income you may want to itemize it on a separate sheet and simply list the total below.

GROSS SALARY (primary employer)   _____
Include money taken out for taxes, retirement
Contributions (both yours and your employer), health care premium
Contributions (both yours and your employer)

GROSS SALARY (secondary employer)   _____
Include money taken out for taxes, retirement
Contributions (both yours and your employer), health care premium
Contributions (both yours and your employer)

OTHER INCOME   _____
Alimony, child support, rental income,
temporary jobs, disability, commissions

GIFTS RECEIVED (financial)   _____

INTEREST (savings accounts, stocks, bonds)   _____

RETIREMENT PAYOUTS (SS, employer, 401k's,   _____
403b's, IRA'S)

           GROSS INCOME   _____

INCOME STATEMENT CONTINUED

Now take your total from the previous page. Divide gross annual income by 12 to get your monthly income and by 52 to get your weekly income.

Total Gross Yearly Income from previous page   _____

Total Gross Monthly Income   _____

Total Gross Weekly Income   _____

Gross expenses prior to take-home pay. Divide annual expenses by 12 to get your monthly expenses and by 52 to get your weekly expenses.

Gross expenses prior to take-home pay = all taxes paid (federal, state, local, and payroll) + health insurance premiums + retirement account contributions

Total Gross Yearly Expenses   _____

Total Gross Monthly Expenses   _____

Total Gross Weekly Expenses   _____

[Net Income = Gross Income – Gross Expenses]

Now, looking simply at your Net Incomes:

Total Net Yearly Income   _____

Total Net Monthly Income   _____

Total Net Weekly Income   _____

When looking at our expenses on a weekly, monthly, or annual basis it is important that we be able to compare them to our income both gross and net. If we look at them only on one level it is possible to believe that there is not enough, both because of large bills that need to be paid only once or twice a year, and because we are not totally accounting for all that we actually receive. It is also important when managing our spending that we understand what our net weekly, monthly, and annual income is so that we do not overspend unintentionally.

It is also VERY important to remember that this is a number and it is NOT who you are. I have had a member in my class whose Net Worth was $7.00 and they were amazingly prosperous. I have had individuals whose net worth was in the millions and they were worried about not having enough.

An Integral Approach to:

Creating Sustainable Prosperity!

Chapter 7

Fear, Lack & Scarcity

Values Based Allocation of Money

FEAR, LACK & SCARCITY

Using and understanding money represents a very large fear for many people. We have bought into the idea that it is complicated and that we cannot fully understand it. Yet we all earn money and spend money. It is a requirement of living in the modern world that we take ownership of our finances and release our fears around money.

In his book *Prosperity*, Charles Fillmore states:

> *Fear is a great breeder of poverty, for it breaks down positive thoughts. Negative thoughts bring negative conditions in their train. The first thing to do in making a demonstration of prosperity in the home is to discard all negative thoughts and words. Build up a positive thought atmosphere in the home, an atmosphere that is free from fear and filled with love. Do not allow any words of poverty or lack to limit the attractive power of love in the home. Select carefully only those words that charge the home atmosphere with the idea of plenty, for like attracts like in the unseen as well as the seen. Never make an assertion in the home, no matter how true it may look on the surface that you would not want to see persist in the home.[xxxv]*

These words carry even more power when we consider that they were written during the Depression. The challenges that many of us have faced after our "crash" in 2008 are minimal when we consider the combined effects of the stock market crash and the Dust Bowl on American life during the early '30's. Again, as with so many truth teachings, this seems contrary to "the facts" as our intellect sees them. Dealing with this truth requires us to operate from a deeper level of truth. We must move to Second Tier consciousness, spiritual adulthood, to hold disparate ideas in our mind at once. When you can do that you will find the truth in both, and at the same time move into prosperity consciousness in the face of apparent lack or scarcity.

When we are in financial fear it is our subjective experience of an objective fact. It is our story about what is happening for us financially that actually brings about the fear. In the summer of 1994, after my mother's death at the end of April, my ordination in June at Unity Village, and my divorce in July, my 16-year-old son and I were driving west to Denver from Fayetteville, Arkansas, to start a new life (my 18-year-old daughter would join us in a few months). We arrived to stay as guests in a borrowed apartment until we could find a place of our own. I had told Jeff that I would buy a house where he wanted to go to school, which would give him some feeling of control over his rapidly changing life.

We arrived in Denver in a pouring rainstorm our headlights were on in the middle of the late afternoon, and our wipers on full power. We were only barely able to see the road. We were looking for an address that we had been to once before during a previous exploratory trip in a new city. After arriving feeling totally exhausted and spent, we unloaded the car and walked into the apartment that would be our home for the next three months. The rain then stopped and Jeff wanted to go and look at the area of town we had chosen from a book that we had that described and evaluated high schools in the area. He thought he wanted a small school that would allow him to play basketball, a passion of his at age 16. Pre GPS and MapQuest, we had our physical fold-out map and book in hand as we set out to find the area.

We were moving from fear and exhaustion to being excited to be looking at where we might eventually live. After the stress of our earlier drive we felt that this would be fun way to relax and to place ourselves in a positive mindset. We might even be finding our new home as we drove and saw homes for sale. We were ready to look for "for sale" signs. It was a shock to arrive in the neighborhood. It turned out to be a very poor area of the city with run down homes, weedy lots, and with trash everywhere. Given the stress of drive into Denver and the last few weeks we almost simultaneously burst into tears. Jeff asked in total seriousness if we were going to "have to live in a box," his was of way of saying, "Were we going to be homeless?" "Were we going to have to live in a ghetto?" Now, that was a groundless fear but we both tapped into it at the same time. His father was very generous to us, so that was not really going to happen, but it was totally how we both felt in that moment.

This is a wonderful example of the teaching, "we are not our feelings." Feelings are just something that we have, they come and they go, and they are not real. It was our subjective experience resulting from accumulated stress and exhaustion. It was a financial fear that felt totally real in that moment and it felt like an objective fact as we drove the streets of that neighborhood that we had chosen from a book. We discovered that it was not what we dreamed it would be, and we really had no idea where to go next. Where we would live if this was not this place? Maria Nemeth says,

> *Scarcity [fear] is our interpretation, [it is] what we draw from our discomfort of encountering a limit. How do we learn from it? First, we must face our fear. The moment you face your fear and tell the truth about your experience of scarcity, it loses its potency. Then you can move on to its lesson of the limitation it represents. Each time we confront scarcity we learn something from it. This prompts us to develop, or evolve, our human potential and our consciousness.*"[xxxvi]

The feelings of fear, scarcity, and lack destroy us every time we allow ourselves to go into those feelings, into that energy and stay there. When we go there it is often a result of our context from our family and our history with significant others. Rising above those thoughts to holding our own knowing about our worthiness and value is a significant part of the work of the rest of our life.

Having experienced or declared Chapter 7, 11, or 13 in our history often impacts how we feel about money. Having overwhelming debt, working for years at low paying jobs, or not working at all, whether we have degrees or not, all impact our beliefs about money and our ability to have enough to survive, let alone "more than enough." The way we spend money, handle money, or save money are all impacted by our knowing, or lack of knowing, that there is always more than enough. They also impact our knowing that we are worth significant salaries and successful ways of being in this world. They impact our reaction to the word successful... whether we are even willing to own what we want and whether we deserve to be successful. For every day, hour, or even minute that we spend giving credence to doubt, fear, or worrying about our futures we diminish our ability to create the abundance we would like to have in our lives.

Wallace Wattles, in his classic book, *Think and Grow Rich*, puts it this way, "If you want to become rich, you must not make a study of poverty. Things are not brought into being by thinking about their opposite."[xxxvii] Often the context of our lives is a "study of poverty".

We must consciously choose to let go of that context and all of the accompanying baggage in order to have sustainable prosperity. We can develop a combination of spending and saving that takes into account our values and that also allows us to choose consciously and deliberately what kinds of things we spend money on and what kinds of things we invest our lives in by spending our precious life force to fund them. Nemeth says, "We all have a limited time here on earth. We all have limited energy. The question for many of us is *not* 'how can I get more?' Instead, the question is: What miracles can I perform with what I have."[xxxviii]

Getting into the mindset of seeing the miracles of what we have rather than the fear and scarcity that we project with our minds into our lives allows us to bring the Divine into our current lives. From seeing what we have in our current lives we can multiply or project that into even more, thus creating successful, prosperous lives for ourselves and for our families. When we are in the framework of fear, worry, and lack, we only project that into the future, creating more "same old… same old". Many of us fear and are repulsed by folks with money. We attribute success to greed and dishonesty. Again, we are called to make a distinction.

Nemeuth quotes "John Maynard Keynes offers a wonderful quotation that plays on this theme, putting it into perspective: The love of money as a possession—as distinguished from the love of money as a means to the enjoyments and realities of life—should be recognized for what it is, a somewhat disgusting morbidity, one of those semi-criminal, semi-pathological propensities which one hands over with a shudder to the specialists in mental disease."[xxxix] Loving money as a means to the enjoyments and realities of life, is one of our paths out of fear about money and having "too much" money. Money is a tool that allows us to put our values and our desires into practice. We can all be multi-millionaires and live exactly in the way that we choose.

Look at Warren Buffet as an example. He is one of the richest men on the planet. He lives in the same small town in Omaha, Nebraska, that he has always lived in. He lives in the same house that he raised his children in, before he was a multi-billionaire. He has the money to support the things that he believes in and live in the way that he chooses to live. Many of us fear becoming Donald Trump. We need not have that fear if we are living by our values and spending our money from those values; none of that changes, no matter how large the figure at the top of our monthly income statement. It matters not if it $1,000 a month, $10,000 a month, or $100,000 or more a month. Often our real fear is of **having money** rather than **not having money** because it may be familiar to us to not have money. Having money can be the source from which our fear springs. For those of us who fear poverty we can then see the miracle in what we have and see it expanding to more than fulfill our needs while we prudently spend what we have.

How can that be? More money never fills the hole created by our experience of not having enough. We all know the stories of folks that win the lottery and end up badly in debt and losing everything. We also know the stories of millionaires who pinch every penny they have and live in poverty dying with unspent millions. Scarcity and lack is an experience arising from our feelings, not from the facts. One way we create those feelings is by comparing ourselves to others. There is always going to be someone who "appears" richer than you or poorer than you. Living by trying to "keep up with the Joneses" is a sure way to live in a feeling of scarcity and lack. Being embarrassed by what you have is another way to limit your sustainable prosperity.

When we do not feel worthy of the success we have attained we will often lose it. Not because we are unworthy, not because we do not deserve it, but because we "feel" like we are unworthy, "we feel" that we do not deserve it. We then communicate that belief into the Universe and that belief helps us by removing the success that we are projecting with our feelings that we do not want. Sometimes we are the most successful person in our families. Think of Oprah Winfrey, for example. She has often publically shared how much she has given to her family that has unfortunately been much under-appreciated and wasted. She has to allow her success to be hers, to keep it. While she struggled with that concept at the very beginning of her success, she has gradually overcome her misgivings as her success has materially grown.

Nemeth teaches that, "Comparisons are knee jerk responses. Trying to stop them is useless. On the contrary, it is important that you recognize and identify these responses. Make them conscious. The comparisons you make between yourself and other people often reflect your current life's lessons."[xl] Remember, if our buttons are pressed, that they are our buttons and those that press them are our teachers. When our buttons are pressed then and only then do we have an opportunity to heal that issue, therefore removing the button. Most of us will never remove them all. But as the thoughts arise we can choose to look at them, see them, and then let them go, without them having significant and detrimental impacts on our ongoing lives.

This additional quote from Nemeth is worth noting:

> Do you try to avoid scarcity? Do you manipulate yourself into thinking it does not exist by rationalizing away your feelings: 'I'm being overly sensitive?' Do you misuse positive thinking strategies or affirmations? Unfortunately, the more you run, and focus attention on avoiding your feelings, the faster the fire-breathing Dragon of Scarcity catches up with you. You have the capacity to know yourself better by looking at the ways scarcity works in your life, and at how to live more fully as a human being. Your life will become full of adventures instead of defenses.[xli]

As we go forward to create our Money Allocation Sheet, a budget to most folks, I invite us to do so without a mindset of fear, lack, or scarcity. We simply allocate the income we have in alignment with OUR VALUES. From that place we know that there is more than enough to do the things that are ours to do. As we see that top number, our income increasing, we can know exactly where we would like to put that money to bring forth more of our values into our lives and into our world. We release limiting thoughts and behaviors... Remembering that 'Perfect love casts out fear,' I John 4:18.

You have already attributed values to the items that you spend your money on. Now simply put them on the appropriate line. Then you can go back to page 102 and complete your values work.

BASED ON MY VALUES

_____I CHOOSE THE FOLLOWING WAYS TO ALLOCATE MY MONEY:

NAME

This is your worksheet. We will create a final version later. **Do this in pencil and have your eraser handy.**

My weekly Net Income: $_____

Look at your six weeks of cash purchases and average those amounts into a cash purchases per week, leaving out any extraordinary one-time expense that might have occurred. (May belong in categories below)

$_____

Now look at your discretionary and non-discretionary expenses over the last six weeks. List them by categories. There are some listed below. Feel free to add others or leave a category blank if it does not apply to you. Look at the value represented by each category. Notice if there is a category that you did not spend money on in the last six weeks that should be included, i.e. vacation. Be sure to include it now. Consult your desires and any financial requirements. Make sure that you have included them and the estimate of what they will require on a monthly basis.

	VALUE	AMOUNT
Auto	_____	
Fuel		_____
Insurance		_____
Loan		_____
Registration		_____
Service/Maintenance		_____
Business Expenses	_____	_____
Charity (Giving)	_____	_____
Clothing	_____	_____
Computer (Technology)	_____	_____
Education	_____	_____
Entertainment (Recreation)	_____	_____
Gifts Given	_____	_____
Groceries	_____	_____
Housing	_____	
HOA Fees		_____
Insurance		_____

Mortgage/Rent   _____

Mortgage Insurance   _____

Utilities

     Cable TV   _____

     Garbage & Recycling   _____

     Gas & Electric   _____

     Internet   _____

     Telephone(s)   _____

     Water   _____

Insurance   _____

     Disability   _____

     Life   _____

     Medical   _____

Interest Expense   _____   _____

IRA (Retirement Contribution   _____   _____

Medical   _____

     Doctors   _____

     Medicine   _____

Misc.   _____

Personal Care   _____   _____

Pets   _____   _____

Savings   _____   _____

Tax   _____

     City   _____

     Federal   _____

     State   _____

     Medicare   _____

     SDI

     Social Security   _____

Vacation   _____   _____

         Total   _____

An Integral Approach to:

Creating Sustainable Prosperity!

Chapter 8

Forgiveness & Releasing

FORGIVENESS

Releasing and forgiveness are both such simple words to say, yet such difficult concepts to embrace and practice in our daily lives in a simple manner. The distinction between easy and simple needs to be practiced and repeated again, and again, and again because simple is almost never easy. We actually can learn how to accept ourselves, to accept our lives as perfect, just exactly the way that they are in this very moment. We need to stop withholding and being embarrassed by anything in our past, anything that we have ever done, and anything that has ever been done to us.

We work it, and work it, and work it, until we reach this place of knowing that our lives, and the lives of everyone we have ever known, have been brought together in a truly perfect way, so that we could learn the lessons that we signed up to learn in this life, on a soul level. We might as well begin with the big ones, shame and guilt. Every little thing you have ever done that you are embarrassed by, you need to simply cough it up. It is really very similar to what you have probably watched as you watched a cat cough up a hair ball. We start out by gagging on the process. We may even feel like vomiting a little in the process, but what we are doing is totally freeing the passageways of our breathing. We cough them up, one by one, as they come up, and when we are finally finished we can breathe freely and openly, allowing the breath of Spirit to cleanse every cell in our bodies.

We reach the point where we are willing to "confess" to anyone – because the idea that it is inappropriate for us to communicate everything that we have ever done that can be construed as negative that can be linked to feelings of shame, embarrassment, and guilt. We learn to share in appropriate places and contexts, and we are willing to share anytime it will serve another.

We can start with the little hair balls. Yes, when I was six or 10 or 15, I stole from the dime store, the Walgreens, the local grocery store. There, it is better is it not? Yes, I cheated on tests, Yes, I have a police record, yes, I am an alcoholic, yes, I overeat, yes, I feel powerless to change my life, yes, I need help. Once we get past the little hairballs we can move on to sexual indiscretions, or drinking, or bankruptcies, or even criminal records, and just say what it was we did in the past. We can make amends if necessary, and then let it go.

Whether we are gay or straight, whether we are divorced or have always been single, whether we have more degrees than we know what to do with, or whether we never graduated from high school. Who we are in this moment is exactly who we are, and we can choose to accept that about ourselves; when we can accept that about ourselves a miracle happens.

We can start by accepting ourselves and forgiving ourselves whatever we have done, just as we are in this very moment. When we have started the process of accepting ourselves THEN we are able to begin choosing how we will be from this moment forward. When we can find compassion for ourselves then compassion and unconditional love for others is only a small step away. Then we can begin to forgive all of the people who have disappointed us, who have let us down, who did not live up to our expectations, and then we are can finally be free at last, "praise God Almighty, we're free at last." That is the goal. That is what happens when we can finally calm our egos down enough to actually begin the process. That is what happens when we can accept that this is who we are, that this is who our mothers, fathers, spouses, lovers, brothers and sisters, uncles and aunts, grandparents, teachers, and everyone else with whom we have ever come into contact really are; then, and only then, can we truly be at peace.

The truly amazing thing is that we simply have to be willing. We do not have to know everything about how the forgiveness process will unfold. The *how* presents itself when we have conquered our block of un-willingness. The how will become easy when we are willing to admit that we want to take advantage of the peace that is promised us when we finally take the plunge and begin to forgive, sometimes one hairball at a time. Another often-asked question is how will I know that I have forgiven everything, everyone that I need to forgive?

You will have given up all of your stories. You will have given up all of the stories about all of the people that have "done you wrong." You will have no issue with them. You may not ever choose to be their best friend, but the sight of them coming toward you on the street, in a store, or at a family gathering, will be a non-event. You will even be willing to go up and hug them and ask how they are doing... and really want to hear the answer.

What you are really saying is, "This is who I was, and I'm not that anymore." Or you are saying, "This is who they were (maybe even still are), but I have compassion for them because if we or they could have done it better we/they would have, or if they could do it better in this very moment they would."

There is another important factor that must be addressed. It is very important to remember that forgiveness **DOES NOT MEAN STUFFING YOUR FEELINGS, OR "MAKING NICE",** with abusive bullies, or even unkind people. Feel your feelings. Acknowledge your anger but then let it go. You do not have to become anyone's best friend, hang out with them, or spend hours on the phone with them. However, again, you will not have to avoid them, and you no longer have them living in your head rent free. You can deal with them as you would deal with any other casual acquaintance with no attachment to what they say or do. If you find that you are getting attached to your past pain or their current actions, remind yourself that you have forgiven them and simply let go... again... and again... of the story that arises. Think of forgiveness as peeling an onion. Layer by layer we let go until there is nothing left but peelings -- and then we get rid of those in the garbage.

I mentioned at the beginning of this book, I have taught nearly every prosperity class that I am aware exists. All of those classes teach a primary lesson, that in order to be truly prosperous, we have to forgive. Charles Fillmore in his book *Prosperity* says it this way: "This means that we must cultivate a love for our fellows in order to set the attractive force of love into operation... As love attracts, hate dissipates. Before you approach God's altar of plenty, go and make friends with your brother(s). Make friends even with the money powers. Do not envy the rich. Never condemn those who have money merely because they have it and you do not. Do not question how they got their money and wonder whether or not they are honest. All of that is none of your business."[xlii] I love that he says it this way, because it must have been the same in his time as it is in ours. Many of those who are billionaires seem to have less integrity than we would like to see. But, guess what? We even get to forgive them. If we want to be prosperous, and to have abundance in our world, in order to achieve that desire, and in fact all of our desires, we get to be at peace with everyone in the world, rich and poor alike. ...good and not so good.

When I think of learning to love what is in our lives I think of the work of Byron Katie. When I think of forgiveness work I think of Colin Tipping's *Radical Forgiveness*. His first book, and the successive books that he has written concerning the processes that he created, are invaluable in practical forgiveness work. While each of us can set an intention, and begin to work on the process, some of us have to do major work on major items. That is what Colin's work offers: *"To transform energies we must experience them totally, working through them and forgiving them, which means seeing the perfection in them."* In *Radical Forgiveness: Making Room for the Miracles:* "Forgiveness is the *inner* work that we do to increase our experience of freedom. It brings us consciously into the World of Divine Truth. In the World of Humanity, we also need accountability, responsibility for our actions, systems of justice, mediation, reconciliation, treatment programs, jails and prisons. This is the *outer* work of living together in an unenlightened society. These inner and outer levels are connected, yet distinct."[xlii]

Almost all of us have wounds that need to heal. We cannot skip over the work that is needed to release this pain out of our minds, hearts, and bodies. It takes us from isolation, from fear and pain, all the way back home to the Truth of our being, the Truth of who we truly are. Tipping continues, "When you do the inner work of forgiveness, remember that you are not trying to fix yourself, another person, or a situation. You are not looking for justice in order to champion injustice. You are not a savior or a victim or a perpetrator. Those are roles that you constructed. You are not bound by them, nor is anyone else." This is a big step for us to take. To move to the place of seeing the learning, and even the blessings in our painful past, is the hero's journey of mythology. As you make this hero's journey you can release the need to blame, to shame, or to seek revenge upon anyone else, including yourself.

What are the benefits of forgiving someone?

Research results cited here come from the renowned Mayo Clinic in Minnesota. For more information, go to www.mayoclinic.com. Researchers have recently become interested in studying the effects of forgiveness. Evidence is mounting that holding on to grudges and bitterness results in long-term health problems. Forgiveness, on the other hand, offers numerous benefits, including:

> Lower blood pressure
> Stress reduction
> Less hostility
> Better anger management skills
> Lower heart rate
> Lower risk of alcohol or substance abuse
> Fewer depression symptoms
> Fewer anxiety symptoms
> Reduction in chronic pain
> More friendships

Healthier relationships

Greater religious or spiritual well-being

Improved psychological well-being

Who do we need to forgive? We need to forgive anyone or any situation that comes to mind where there is any pain involved for us. We start with the ones that loom largest in our minds every day. We move to the ones that set us off anytime we think of them. We move on to those that have wronged us somehow, even if we no longer hold bad feelings against them. Sometimes we have not been aware enough to know the ways that we have been hurt or damaged by those in our past. Maybe they ruined our reputation, convinced us to take needless risks, possibly physical, financial, or illegal.

I am guessing that you may now have a long list. Feel free to begin by writing a list of those that you are choosing to forgive. Do not forget to add yourself to the list. Most of us have made decisions in our lives that affected us in many hurtful ways. Sometimes the ramifications of our past decisions have damaged our own lives in major ways. A good test to conduct, if it comes to your mind then write it down, and then do some forgiveness work around it. I have included six sheets in the book. You can also create a forgiveness journal, and work with these questions in great depth.

[Working the 12 Steps is also one of the good ways to arrive at the forgiveness work that is yours to do. A copy of the 12 Steps is in the Appendix.]

MY PHYSICAL ENVIRONMENT

As you reflect on the statements below, they invite you to notice how you feel about your home, your office space, your office equipment, and your organization. Whether you have a small apartment or a spacious house, how you feel in that space reflects on your prosperity. One of the most important statements below is, "I easily let go of items that no longer serve a purpose in my home, office, and/or life." Things that you no longer wear, use, or enjoy need to be released and used by someone who wants or needs them. Clean your drawers, closets, and files. Putting it away, selling it, giving it away, or throwing it away, will go a long way to increasing your prosperity and enjoyment of your home.

_____I live in a home that I love.

_____The things in my home are a reflection of me and my values.

_____My home and surroundings are a haven for my soul.

_____I surround myself with beautiful things.

_____People feel relaxed and peaceful in my home.

_____There is ample and healthy lighting around me.

_____I am not tolerating anything about my home environment.

_____I surround myself with sounds that make my life more enjoyable (music, silence or other pleasing acoustics).

_____My bedroom lets me have the best sleep possible (bed, covers, light and air)

_____I have the support that I need to fully maintain my home, car and workspace (cleaning help, mechanic, and handy person).

_____I sort the mail and place it where it belongs when I come into my home and/or office.

_____My home is clean and tidy (closets, cupboards and drawers organized, desks and tables clear, furniture in good repair, windows clean).

_____My appliances, machinery and equipment work well, (fridge, toaster, lawn mower, water heater, etc.).

_____I am a responsible steward of my environment, practicing the principle to reduce, recycle and reuse.

_____My personal files, papers and receipts are neatly filed away.

_____My clothes enhance my appearance (not worn out, or ill-fitting clothes).

_____I have nothing around my home, office or in storage that I do not love or need.

_____I easily let go of items that no longer serve a purpose in my home, office and/or life.

RELEASING STUFF

My experience with the individuals that I have worked with is that those with a lot of forgiveness work to do often have an opportunity to release much more than their stories from the past. Our lives and our homes are symbolic of our emotional state. I have found working with people over the past twenty years that this can be a chicken and egg kind of process. We work with forgiveness, letting go of our emotional baggage, AND we work with cleaning the clutter out of our lives. Or we can begin with the process of editing our possessions, choosing to keep only those things that we consistently use or that we love. When we are totally honest with ourselves we find that most of the things that "overstuff" our lives do not really fall into either of those categories.

If we share our life with others, please keep in mind that WE ARE ONLY IN CHARGE OF OUR STUFF. Releasing other's stuff is only going to give us more forgiveness work to do. This can be a challenge when we are on a different page than others we live with. It seems that sometimes, however, the effort can be contagious—as we clean up our own areas then, somehow, our family members may respond with a similar behavior. Reminding all of us that offering to work **with** our children or spouses, often creates better results than demanding that they **clean up their stuff**.

As I prepared to downsize from a 3,800 sq. ft. home with an oversized garage and lots of basement storage to boot, and move to a 1,400 sq. ft. condo, I found out again that it was a process. It was a process that involved looking at, touching, and personally handling each item, while I simultaneously asked myself the following kinds of questions. You may think of more relevant questions to add.

When is the last time I used, wore, or even looked at this? Why do I still have it?
If it had been years since I even looked at it, then it dawned on me to question why I still had the possession in the first place. I will use the example of china. I had my paternal grandmother's Havilland china. It was a Greek key pattern in gold and black. It was beautiful, I had a setting for twelve people, with only a couple of pieces broken, but essentially it was all there with extra platters, serving dishes, and tiny teacups and saucers. Fortunately, or unfortunately, I never used it.

My daughters didn't want the china set. I did not want it, but for some mysterious reason I had moved it from Swanton, Ohio, to Cleveland, Ohio, to Erie, Pennsylvania, to Fayetteville, Arkansas, to Denver, Colorado, and then back to Cincinnati, Ohio. I had created places to store it but I never used it. I also had my mother's fine china, pieces of my maternal grandmother's fine china, and the Dalton china I had bought for my hope chest as a teenager. My personal style does not include fine china or delicate crystal. With much angst I finally decided to sell it all. Not surprisingly, I have never missed it. It was not a good market for china, so I did not make much money from the sale, but, PRAISE GOD, I was free.

What do you have that you have carried with you for your whole life that falls into this category?

Clothes are another thing. Those of us that did not have a lot of material possessions as we were growing up seem to think that having closets, dressers, and chests of drawers that are overflowing brings us a feeling of abundance. It is a false feeling. Just as pictures of happy families in albums do not create happy family memories, bulging closets and cupboards do not make us prosperous. We all know the tests, but do we really do it? Have you worn it in a year? If not, sell it, or give it away to friends, Good Will, or to the Salvation Army. Does it fit? If not, sell it, or give it away. If you buy something new take a comparable piece from your closet to give away or sell. Do not let the "stuff" multiply and overtake your life. Just as we have watched how we spend our money we can now begin to watch how we accumulate stuff and choose very carefully what stuff we keep, what we choose to release, and what we add to our collection. Watching both our spending and our collecting will allow us to also watch the "stuff" we add to our emotional baggage and how we can release it as well.

Can I find it if I want it?

Once you have begun the process of editing or releasing the things that no longer serve you, the next task at hand is to organize your things so that you can easily find them when you want them. This applies to every place you put things in your home. Closets, are they organized by season, by color, by casual and professional? Linen closets, can you easily pick out the towel, beach towel, extra blankets, or pillows, without having to take out everything in the closet to get to what you want? Kitchen cupboards, are yours clean and arranged carefully? Are your cupboards overrun with plastic take out, frozen food containers from frozen dinners and plastic silverware from take out? Recycle what you can and throw out the rest.

Plastic bags and take out containers are another plague. Take them back to the store and use your own bags that you take with you to stores to avoid their re-growth, re-cycle the containers. Are your drawers sorted? Are your important papers filed? Are your books... the paper ones... arranged so that you can easily locate the ones that you want? It is not necessary to be anal about it but putting them in some kind of order creates order and peace in your life. When you keep only what is important to you, that you love, your life becomes simpler and simplicity is the beginning of sustainable prosperity.

"And this mess is so big, And so deep and so tall, We cannot pick it up. There is no way at all!" — Dr. Seuss, *The Cat in the Hat*

I know that feeling, and I am guessing as you start this project that you may feel this way as well. Having faced and conquered this task, and as I continue to refine my things, edit them if you will, I have found that it is easiest to start small, declare a small victory, and move to another small project until, suddenly, you can see the progress you are making and you become inspired to continue onto yet another project.

Make a commitment to clean out one drawer. Decide what the purpose of that drawer is, what goes in there? Then take EVERYTHING out of that drawer and do not put anything back that does not belong there. You may choose to put the leftovers into a box [**if it is something you love or use and are going to keep**], if not recycle it or throw it away now. I know that leaves you with a pile in the box that you do not know what to do with. If you have the time and energy to choose another drawer, then decide which drawer that will be. Repeat the process. Does anything in your box go into that drawer? If not add to the box, the recycle pile, or the trash. Notice that you have successfully made a dent. Keep up the process until you live in the home that you want to live in.

In line with this section, once you have used it put it away. Especially in the clean drawers, cupboards, closets, etc. The further you get in this process the easier it becomes. Once everything has a place it is easier to use it and put it back in the place. I know, I know, I know, your mother told you this years ago… some of the things she tried to teach you were worth learning… Thanks Mom!

Is anyone in my family going to want to inherit this?

Okay, let us assume you **LOVE** this thing. **IT** is big, **IT** is awkward, and **IT** takes up the whole room. You plan whole rooms around **IT**. At some point in your life, you have to ask yourself if you still really want **IT**. **IF,** and this is a big **IF,** none of your heirs will really want it you are doing them a favor to sell **IT** or give **IT** away to someone else who will really **LOVE IT**—rather than having your heirs stuck knowing what to do with **IT,** eventually setting it out on the curb in despair. I know that this is the farthest thing on some of your minds right now, while for others it is something you think about and live with daily. Either way, this is a sustainable prosperity tip for now and on into the future.

An additional personal example that I had to deal with for years was a five-foot-long, four-foot-high, roll-top desk with chair, which my father bequeathed me as I entered into adulthood. It was oak and the latest technology when he bought it long, long, long before I was born. It sat in our library when I lived with him, and it sat there after I no longer lived there, until I had to put him in a retirement home. Like the china, I moved it to all of those places I mentioned before. It was a prominent feature in every home the family occupied. Not having had much of a real relationship with my father, I developed a relationship with the things that he owned (I still live with lots of them). He had good taste. He predicted that his grandchildren would fight over his things (he was wrong… none of them want them). I have also sold the desk. They will not have to deal with that.

Notice that I am telling you that my relationship with my father was lacking in all of the ways I would have liked to be in relationship with my father. I had to forgive my father knowing again that he had done the best that he could. My substitute relationship with my father's things was never going to meet my little-girl needs. As I began to release the things that were my father's it helped my forgiveness process. Going back to the layers of an onion, I forgave, I released — I released and I forgave. When we look at these processes as part of our stage development in an integral healing process we can begin to look backward at the contexts of our lives, and notice every opportunity to continue the healing process. There are a few things that were my father's that I will probably leave to my children to get rid of because I use them every day. However, I am at peace with my father's memory and I feel a healing in that area of my life.

Your home should be a retreat for you. A place that makes you feel good. Even thinking about being there should make you feel good, warm, and safe. It does not mean that you have to meet some external standard of style. It should meet your personal, internal standard of aesthetics. You should think it is attractive, beautiful, and comforting. It should feed your soul. Think about the beauty that you are creating as you edit your things. You will be surrounded by the things you use and love.

Releasing the "stuff" of your life creates healing, forgiveness and, yes, sustainable prosperity.

LETTING GO

Forgiveness and releasing are about letting go. Whether we are talking about emotional baggage from our pasts or the dress we wore to our Junior Prom or the football jersey we wore in Junior High. We are talking about moving to and living in the present moment. It is this moment that contains all of the beauty, pain, and life that is present here because you are here. We cannot reclaim the past nor should we want to. The future will not happen any sooner because we want it to. This moment, our home, our environment, our current relationships receive priority when we can let go of everything that is not happening now. Simply look at your hands? Are they clenched? If they are, consciously open them. Let go of whatever you are holding onto and allow yourself to be free… free at last.

Forgiveness

This forgiveness sheet is to work with my issues regarding_____.

_____, (name of person you are forgiving) I forgive you for: (your story about what they did wrong)

_____

_____

_____

_____

_____

_____

_____

_____

_____

_____

_____

_____

_____

I am also grateful to you (the person that you are forgiving) because I have received _?_ from this experience and that has furthered my spiritual evolution:

_____

_____

_____

_____

_____

_____

I know that I also disappointed you. (How what you disappointed the person you are forgiving; you are asking their forgiveness) Please forgive me for:

_____

_____

_____

_____

Forgiveness

This forgiveness sheet is to work with my issues regarding_____.

_____, (name of person you are forgiving) I forgive you for: (your story about what they did wrong)

_____
_____
_____
_____
_____
_____
_____
_____
_____
_____
_____
_____
_____
_____

I am also grateful to you (the person that you are forgiving) because I have received_?_ from this experience and that has furthered my spiritual evolution:

_____
_____
_____
_____
_____
_____
_____

I know that I also disappointed you. (How what you disappointed the person you are forgiving; you are asking their forgiveness) Please forgive me for:

_____
_____
_____
_____

Forgiveness

This forgiveness sheet is to work with my issues regarding_____.

_____, (name of person you are forgiving) I forgive you for: (your story about what they did wrong)

_____
_____
_____
_____
_____
_____
_____
_____
_____
_____
_____
_____
_____

I am also grateful to you (the person that you are forgiving) because I have received_?_ from this experience and that has furthered my spiritual evolution:

_____
_____
_____
_____
_____
_____

I know that I also disappointed you. (How what you disappointed the person you are forgiving; you are asking their forgiveness) Please forgive me for:

_____
_____
_____
_____

Forgiveness

This forgiveness sheet is to work with my issues regarding_____.

_____, (name of person you are forgiving) I forgive you for: (your story about what they did wrong)

_____
_____
_____
_____
_____
_____
_____
_____
_____
_____
_____
_____
_____
_____
_____

I am also grateful to you (the person that you are forgiving) because I have received_?_ from this experience and that has furthered my spiritual evolution:

_____
_____
_____
_____
_____
_____

I know that I also disappointed you. (How what you disappointed the person you are forgiving; you are asking their forgiveness) Please forgive me for:

_____
_____
_____
_____

Forgiveness

This forgiveness sheet is to work with my issues regarding_____.

_____, (name of person you are forgiving) I forgive you for: (your story about what they did wrong)

_____

_____

_____

_____

_____

_____

_____

_____

_____

_____

_____

_____

_____

I am also grateful to you (the person that you are forgiving) because I have received _?_ from this experience and that has furthered my spiritual evolution:

_____

_____

_____

_____

_____

_____

_____

I know that I also disappointed you. (How what you disappointed the person you are forgiving; you are asking their forgiveness) Please forgive me for:

_____

_____

_____

_____

An Integral Approach to:

Creating Sustainable Prosperity!

Chapter 9

Gratitude, Miracles, and Grace:

or How to Recognize Simple Abundance & Net Worth

Gratitude, Miracles, and Grace: or How to Recognize Simple Abundance

By briefly looking back over the chapters that we have just covered we will have a better sense of where we now find ourselves regarding money: namely, how and where we spend our money, a clearer understanding of our money history, a better sense of our energy surrounding money, a clear-eyed view of all of our financial obligations, what we truly desire and value, and the knowledge of how what we spend reflects those desires and values. We can now choose to follow faith, to see the *Truth* rather than experience lack and fear. We have identified who we will need to forgive so that we can finally and honestly be free to live a prosperous life. What more you may well ask do I have to do to live a life that is blessed with sustainable prosperity?

We also have to be aware of the lens, or the filter in front of the lens, that we have around being grateful for our lives. Are you in touch with the miracle that you are? The miracle of your very existence? The miracle that you call 'your life'—as you ride this beautiful, blue, green, and white planet through space? It was Albert Einstein who said, "There are only two ways to live your life. One is as though nothing is a miracle. The other is as though everything is a miracle." If you can see the miracle of life that you are and that surrounds you, it is a small step on your journey to living a life of gratitude, a life of abundance, which will be filled with grace.

Wallace Wattles, in *The Science of Getting Rich: The Proven Mental Program to a Life of Wealth*, discusses the effects of the opposite experience of living in gratitude: "Many people who order their lives rightly in all other ways are kept in poverty by their lack of gratitude."[xliii] Perhaps as Truth Students you have practiced all of the prosperity teachings that you have been taught and still abundance eludes you. Wattles' simple statement contains much truth for us today. He goes on to say that "Without gratitude you cannot long keep from dissatisfaction upon things as they are, you begin to lose ground. You fix attention on the common, the ordinary, the poor, and the squalid and mean; and your mind takes the form of these things. Then you will transmit these forms or mental images to the Formless, and the common, the poor, the squalid, and mean will come to you."[xliv]

None of us set out to attract those things into our lives. However, when we are unaware of our context, our money history, we can easily fall into the mental habits of our human heritage, and be unable to move beyond them. He also says that "The grateful mind is constantly fixed upon the best; therefore it tends to become the best; it takes the form or character of the best, and will receive the best."[xlv] Now, we can take that simply to be material possessions or we can expand that to encompass all of areas of true abundance and *Sustainable Prosperity* in our lives.

Our culture has a tradition of blessing food, based at least in part on the story of Jesus' miracle of feeding the five thousand, as told in three of the gospels, Matthew, Mark and John: "Then Jesus took the loaves and gave thanks. He handed out the bread to those who were seated. He gave them as much as they wanted. And he did the same with the fish." John 6:11. What we see with this example in this story is that when the food was blessed... **THERE WAS MORE THAN ENOUGH!** Remember, either everything is a miracle or nothing is a miracle. Many of us still honor the tradition of blessing our food before we eat. However, I would like to expand our consciousness into blessing our home, our electricity, our heat or cooling, and our clothing, all of which make our lives comfortable.

It is important that we bless everything in our lives, much of which may include inherent positives and negatives. The list can include carbon-based energy sources like the oil and natural gas in the ground the fuel that provides power to our homes and our vehicles. We can even bless the animals that died for our leather shoes and bags, the farmers that grow our fruits and vegetables, the fresh water that we still have readily available to drink, the clean air that we breathe. The list of blessings can be endless. Learning to notice the details and blessings of your life can become a spiritual practice. Perhaps it starts with some of the list just mentioned or with something as simple and beautiful as a perfect red leaf in your path on a bright blue fall day, or the fog in the early morning that highlights the drops of dew that etch the beauty of an intricate spider web stretching through the branches of a tree or a bush on your path, or the child that spontaneously throws their arms around you in greeting, or the expressions of love and tenderness that are given by those you love. These examples can all be prime subjects for the focus of your gratitude.

It is very, very, very meaningful that we notice the blessings that surround us and be grateful for each one. Each moment of grace and beauty that is a part of every hour and every day adds value to our lives. It is important for us to learn to acknowledge the gifts we are given with our eyes, with our thoughts, with our words, and most of all with our hearts. When we stop to mark the beauty of the moment and acknowledge it; we have made huge strides in creating more abundance, more miracles, and more of all that we desire in our lives. Moreover, it is even more important that we record the observations. It is important to give them form and structure so that the Universe will respond by supplying even more. The abundance of the universe is unlimited. The only limit on our share of abundance is our ability to receive and to accept what we are given, and our attitudes as we receive. If we simply take it in stride as our due, we are living as if there are no miracles. If we live as if there are no miracles then there are fewer and fewer miracles, and the grace that flows endlessly through our lives will go past un-noticed and un-recognized perhaps even decreasing.

Charles Fillmore, Co-Founder of Unity, is regarded as the creator of "Gratitude Deposit Slips," which I have been told, were available all over Unity Village. They were designed like a bank deposit sheet and were available so that whenever anyone experienced something meaningful they were there for them to write it down immediately. Those slips could then be deposited in their "Gratitude Account" or "Thanksgiving Account." In these accounts they grew and accrued spiritual interest, creating even more opportunities to record and then deposit more.

Many of us today find it easier to keep a Gratitude Journal. We choose to take the time to write about the things that we are grateful for at the end of each day before we go to bed, or first thing in the mornings, whenever we have our time of reflection and meditation. This Gratitude Journal is invaluable in the times when we are feeling alone and full of despair. We can simply use one of the items that we recorded gratitude for as a focus for our reflection or meditation time. Re-reading our Gratitude Journals not only can bring us comfort and peace, but they also focus our attention on the gifts that we have received. Furthermore, that increased focus and attention on the gifts in our life makes it increasingly likely that we will receive additional gifts from the Universe because we are open and grateful.

In the instructions given for keeping Gratitude Journals we are reminded that it can be even more powerful and meaningful if what we record becomes more than just a list. When I was in elementary school I got my first "locked diary" with a key. I wrote things like, "I got up. I went to school. I came home. I watched TV." The same kinds of lists repeated day after day. I could simply have made ditto marks. Indeed, I found the experience of keeping a diary quite boring despite my excitement and desire to have a diary. Because I didn't really know what to do with the diary, how to record my thoughts and experiences in a meaningful way, the daily practice quickly became a rather boring exercise. Within a matter of weeks, I simply ceased the mundane routine.

The same thing will happen with your practice of gratitude—unless you somehow make the exercise come alive for you. Certainly some of the same things will show up in your journals, but each will be tinged with the nuances of the experience you have on that day. The way the colors of the day are specifically laid out will never be identical. The temperatures, the way the light strikes each situation, are what gives it richness and texture that will differentiate one experience of beauty or love from the next, and they will change from day to day. If expressing your gratitude becomes rote, if you allow it to lose its meaning, the miracles will cease to be experienced and you will stop writing in your journals, just as I stopped writing in my locked diary so very many years ago.

Be sure to notice, savor, and enjoy your life. As you notice and record each beautiful experience you will find them expanding and propelling you toward a more sustainable prosperity. Even though this is a part of the upper-left quadrant, there are now research studies that are beginning to move it toward the upper right quadrant as well. Your own experiences will strengthen that research that is recorded on the coming pages, and it will confirm your own truth. I have found Sarah Ban Breathnach's *Simple Abundance: A Daybook of Comfort and Joy* to be a daily meditation book that beautifully reinforces this experience. I recommend it for you as well. I offer you an excerpt from November 23.

True Thanksgiving

An open home, an open heart,
Here grows a bountiful harvest—Judy Hand

The turkey is in the oven, filling the air with the fragrance of anticipation, and my heart is glad.
The pies are cooling on the rack, overflowing with the fruits of the earth, and my heart is full.
Conversation, companionship, and conviviality transform the rooms of this beloved home, and
my heart is at peace.

Soon dear ones—family and cherished friends—will gather at the table to rejoice in our bounty
of blessings, and with us lift up their hearts in thanksgiving. As the table is set, my heart
gratefully remembers the legacy of love and tradition represented in the talismans of freshly

laundered linens, sparkling crystal, and gleaming china. The silver shines, the candles glow, the flowers delight us with their beauty.

This is good. This is very good. Let us hold fast to this authentic moment of Simple Abundance. Let us cherish this feeling of complete contentment. Let us rejoice and praise the Giver of all good. The English novelist Thomas Hardy believed that the days of declining autumn created an inner season in which we could live 'in spiritual altitudes more nearly approaching ecstasy' than at any other time of the year. Let us exult in our souls' ecstatic accord.

Come, my thankful sisters, come. Offer grace for the bounty of goodness. Raise the song of harvest home, the glass of good cheer, the heart overflowing with joy. We have so much for which to be thankful. So much about which to smile, so much to share. So much, that in this season of plenty, we can embrace the season of relinquishment. All we have is all we need.

O beloved Spirit, truly you have given us so much, an extravagance of riches. Give us, we pray, one thing more. The gift of grateful hearts. Hearts that will not forget what You have done.

One of the reasons that I have chosen the following gratitude exercise is because it was available in the popular media. The truth that Unity teaches has become mainstream in many ways. There isn't an easily traceable path that shows its roots in Unity and yet going back in time shows the primary place it was taught was in Unity and other New Though traditions. Looking for new ways that Truth shows up in the popular media is another source of gratitude for me. I haven't assigned a Gratitude Journal as a part of the homework for this class, however, I RECOMMEND keeping one. This is a practice that you may acquire for yourself.

Giving Thanks: How to Keep a Gratitude Journal

(Good Housekeeping, February 2013)

COMMIT TO HAPPINESS: Journaling is more effective if you first make the conscious decision to become more fulfilled and more grateful. Research suggests, 'Motivation to become happier plays a role**,** Emmons explains.

GO FOR DEPTH OVER BREADTH: Elaborating in detail about a particular thing for which you're grateful—e.g. how thankful you are for your spouse's repair of that broken faucet—carries more benefits than listing many things.

MAKE IT PERSONAL: Focus on people you are grateful for, not things. And try subtraction, not just addition: Reflect on what your life would be like *without* certain blessings rather than just tallying up the good stuff.

SAVOR SURPRISES: Record events that were unexpected or surprising, as these tend to elicit stronger levels of gratitude. For inspiration, search for 'community gratitude journal" at greatergood.berkley.edu.

Behavioral and psychological research has shown the surprising life improvements that can stem from the practice of gratitude.

Two psychologists, Michael McCullough of Southern Methodist University and Robert Emmons of the University of California, wrote an article about an experiment they conducted on gratitude and its impact on well-being. The study split several hundred people into three different groups and all the participants were asked to keep daily dairies. The first group kept a diary of the events without being told specifically to write about either good or bad things; the second group was told to record their unpleasant experiences; and the last group was instructed to make a daily list of things for which they were grateful.

The results of the study indicated that daily Gratitude exercises resulted in higher reported levels of:

Energy
Alertness
Optimism
Enthusiasm
Determination

And further,
those in the gratitude
group were more likely
to: Help others
Exercise more regularly
Experience less depression and stress
Make greater progress toward achieving personal goals

Dr. Emmons says, 'To say we feel grateful is not to say that everything in our lives is necessarily great. It just means we are aware of our blessings.'

I want to acknowledge and thank Unity of Northern Kentucky member, Salle Taft, for the gift of the beautiful, creative, handmade Gratitude Journal that she gave me, and for the above information that she put in my journal. I also want to acknowledge her responsiveness to the promptings of Spirit in giving the journal to me exactly at the time that I needed to write this chapter for *Sustainable Prosperity*. If she would have been able to give the journal to me when she created it, and wanted to present it to me, it might have come too soon. If she would have waited for the "Perfect Time" to give it to me, it would have been too late to be a part of this chapter. She simply brought the journal to church one Sunday and gave it to me in Spirit's time, so that it could be an important part of this book. Salle, I am grateful, thank you!

The grace and miracle of Unity is that which Charles and Myrtle Fillmore began so long ago. The intention with which they began the movement, to simply teach truth that individuals could take into their own homes and churches, although simple in many ways, is profound.

I have not researched Dr. Emmons or his research; he may be a member of a Unity congregation somewhere, but I suspect probably not. Nevertheless, he has researched and given legitimacy to the teachings that Charles presented to the world over a century ago with his "Gratitude Deposit Slips." By focusing on gratitude we will create miracles, insert grace into many situations, and end up blessing our life in untold ways. Perhaps unfairly, Unity never gets a footnote for its contribution to the world of "positive thoughts" and how to bring them into being. Whether it is the above quoted article in *Good Housekeeping* or Norman Vincent Peale's *The Power of Positive Thinking*, which we are told was influenced by Peale's friendship with Eric Butterworth, Unity has, since the late 19th century, quietly spread its message into the world to shape and change the lives of many. For that influence that is influencing and evolving the world and her inhabitants, I am grateful. I would like to give a special Thank You to Charles and Myrtle Fillmore for their vision and intention.

The steps above and the information presented are useless unless practiced. Again, Unity's fifth principle, "We must live the truth that we know," reminds us that to have this step influence our sustainable prosperity we must **use** our Gratitude Journals. Then we can more fully experience the gifts, miracles, and grace of the Universe

Net Worth Worksheet

Instructions

Please remember that this is a snapshot in time at the date the work is completed.

Here's How:

List all of your assets. This includes:

Cash, money held in bank accounts, money market accounts or Certificates of Deposit (CDs)

Personal Property, including homes, cars, boats and recreational vehicles, furniture, art, antiques, collectibles and jewelry

Investments, including stocks, bonds, mutual funds, annuities, the cash value of any life insurance policies and real estate

Retirement Savings, including employee pension plans, 401(k) or 403(b) accounts and IRAs

Then, assign a value to each asset. This should be the estimated resale value of the asset, not what you paid for the item.

Total the value of your assets, and write the resulting figure in the appropriate blank.

List all of your liabilities (debts). This includes: mortgages, home equity loans, car loans, credit cards, bank loans, student loans, personal loans from friends and family, cash advances, medical bills, taxes owed, alimony/child support owed and any other debts that you might have.

Total your liabilities, and write the resulting figure in the "Total Liabilities" field.

Subtract your total liabilities from your total assets. The resulting figure is your current net worth. If the number is positive, you're on the right track. Keep squeezing those pennies and building wealth. If your number is negative, all is not lost. Begin from this moment to build your list of assets.

My Net Worth

Date_____

ASSETS

Cash and Bank Accounts

Cash   _____

Checking   _____

Savings   _____

Other   _____

      Total Cash and Bank Accounts $_____

Investments

401 (k) (b)   _____

IRA   _____

Brokerage Account/Investments   _____

      Total Investments $_____

Other Assets (Estimate)

House(s)   _____

Car(s)   _____

Personal Property   _____

Total Monthly Income (Labor)   _____

Other   _____

      Total Other Assets (Estimate) $_____

      Total Assets $_____

Liabilities

Credit Cards

Credit Card #1 Balance   _____

Credit Card #2 Balance   _____

Credit Card #3 Balance   _____

Credit Card #4 Balance   _____

Other Credit Cards   _____

         Total Credit Card Balance $_____

Other Liabilities

Mortgages(s) (Principal owed)   _____

Student Loan(s) (Principal owed)   _____

Car Loan(s) (Principal owed)   _____

Loans from Family & Friends (Principal Owed)   _____

Total Monthly Bills (Includes interest Payments on Loans)   _____

         Total Other Liabilities $_____

Total Assets $_____

Subtract

Total Liabilities $_____

         Equals

Total Equity/Net Worth $_____

An Integral Approach to:

Creating Sustainable Prosperity!

Chapter 10

Giving, Generously Sharing the Resources We Have Been Given, & Lower Left & Lower Right Quadrants

GENEROUS GIVING

Generous giving is re-gifting what we have already been given. Is that any less a gift because it was first given to you? We give from our excess and it's nearly all excess. This concept becomes much easier when we realize the distinctions between our true desire, needs and wants.

Charles Fillmore said in *Dynamics for Living*, "A gift with reservations is not a gift; it is a bribe." I would also re-write this statement to say, "A gift that is an obligation is not a gift; it is a tax." An obligation is "something that you must do." How many gifts do you give that start with the phrase, "*I have to* buy, to get, to shop for…." In the energy of the Universe no gift that starts out as an obligation really qualifies as giving. Giving starts as a desire to share something that you have with someone else. It starts from a place of compassion and love that wants to express as a gift, no matter what the form the gift takes. It can be an act of service. It can be an item that is given or it can be monetary. It can be money that you have exchanged for a good or service that you then choose, and please notice that 'choose' is the key word here, something that you choose to share with another person or organization.

When it is a true gift there is no transactional exchange in the classic economic sense of giving up something in order to directly receive something else in return. It is not how giving is often expressed in our society or how we were coached by our parents when we were children. We were taught that you will give Joe a Christmas gift and Joe will give you a Christmas present or the reverse. How many times have you received a gift and then you have run out to buy a gift to return because you received one? That is exchange certainly, but it is not giving. Perhaps that is why we often call it a 'Christmas Gift Exchange'. It can be a lot of fun but is it really giving? Another way to look at a gift is as if it is a bribe, "if I give you a gift, then will you be my friend, will you like me, love me, and take care of me?"

Let us go back to the concepts in Chapter 2, *Your Money Story*. Everything is energy. Every "thing" really represents the energy of your life or someone else's life. What are you willing to exchange your life for? When it comes to giving it is very similar. You are exchanging minutes, or hours, of your life energy to give a gift. Are you doing that giving from obligation rather than choice? If so most likely your gift will not really bring blessings into *your* life.

In Chapter 4 we discovered our values and in Chapter 7 we discovered that even when we pay our mortgage or rent we are really expressing one of the values that we hold dear. Giving follows a similar path. We give to what we love. When we only focus on what benefits the giving brings to us it falls under the category of narcissism. Interestingly enough Merriam Webster's online dictionary gives as the first synonym under narcissism "egoism," which expresses the constant source of tension for all of us. Are we living from our essence, from our God-self, from our Divine, from our "individuality" as Emilie Cady expressed it, or are we living from our egos, from our "personalities"? Giving is yet another place where we get to notice how we are expressing in our lives. In Charles Fillmore's *Prosperity* he put it this way, "True giving is the love and generosity of the Spirit quickened heart responding to the love and generosity of the Father's heart." The phrase "the Spirit quickened heart" is, I believe, Fillmore's way of expressing that we are to give from love and compassion, and not from obligation.

In Chapter 1 I quoted Eric Butterworth who taught giving, not necessarily tithing. In the past, when I have taught tithing I have always used the illustration that tithing is simply used as the training wheels for giving. We have dozens of Unity and New Thought teachers teaching how tithing creates abundance for the tither. What they are teaching when applied to conscious, loving giving is absolutely true. When we choose giving first, when we give without fear of lack, amazing abundance will manifest in our lives. It is the structure of the ten percent tithe using the verse in Malachi as a reference that no longer works for me. Again, as I said I have personally given, or tithed, if you will, ten percent from the early nineties to the present. One of Unity's mantras is, "Money comes from expected and unexpected sources." I can give you many, many personal examples of how that principle is valid.

In 1995, as I was co-founding High Country Unity Church in Colorado, we were paying ourselves $100 a week. Starting a church is much like starting a new business. You cannot pull capital out of your business before you have a sustainable and healthy going concern. With my younger daughter in college and my son still in high school, even with their father's generous child support, a $100 a week, was not going to allow me to pay my monthly obligations. Even during this timeframe, I was faithfully giving ten percent of each source of income; my $100 check and my child support. It did not seem to be working the miracles I was hoping for.

Sometime during the second year we and our board were comfortable giving us salaries of $10,000 per year. However, as that number increased the amount of child support decreased. I believe it was shortly after that decrease that fear overcame me and I got a job at a bookstore to help with the expenses. As I was given more and more hours to work I had less and less time for ministry and I realized that working in a bookstore was not compatible with ministry for me. Nor was that check (on which I was also giving) the source of my financial good. After just a few months I gave notice and quit my bookstore job. That *same week* I was asked if I would be willing to drive to the Vail Valley, in Colorado, on Sunday afternoons to help them start a study group. They were willing to pay me more for that service than I had been earning in the bookstore on a weekly basis. Was this a reward for my consistent giving? Is this faith? Is this synchronicity? Is this coincidence? I will leave you to label it what you will. I saw it that way. I still continued 10% giving, I was still making it, and I was still living on faith.

One form that prosperity comes to us is in the form of Divine Ideas that we are then free to act on or not. It was while driving into the mountains on my way up to Vail one Sunday afternoon that I was pondering ways to make more money, in ways that were compatible with my ministerial skill set, and what came to me were the services I had to offer as a minister, like weddings. I could do weddings and with that idea a business was born, ***Weddings at Your Location,*** which consisted of my doing custom weddings in any location, at any time, with any size audience in attendance. Within a year of so I had doubled my income while still giving ten percent of my income.

On another Sunday, when I was the sole minister at High Country, as I received my child support check, I knew that there was not enough money in the church account to pay me, and my mortgage was due. It was going to take most of the child support check to pay the mortgage, and it was time for me to tithe, to write my check to the church. I sat for a very long time, pensively, my pen poised above the blank check. What was I going to do? Write the check and not know where money for the rest of the month was coming from, or keep the money that I needed pay the mortgage and to buy the necessities for my family. Did I believe, really, really, really believe, that giving with joy multiplied what I gave back to me? Could I teach giving if I could not practice it myself? I reached a place of peace and wrote the check and talked about the experience that Sunday morning. An individual in the congregation listened to my story and wrote a generous check to the church on property they had just sold, more than doubling the income to the church for that month, making it possible for the congregation to pay me my salary.

Those of us that have variable sources of income can easily see the effects of percentage giving. I am going to include a story that contributed to my return to giving when fear prevented me from the practice. I had bought a new condo under construction at the height of the housing boom in July of 2008, and I simultaneously put my house on the market in August of 2008, with the fear that my house would sell and close before I could move in November 1st. My house did not sell and I still moved in knowing it would sell soon. When it did not quickly sell I had combined housing payments and utilities that took ninety-plus percent of my net income. I went totally into fear mode and for the first time since 1990 I stopped giving back to the source of my spiritual good. I simply could not afford it is what I told myself. I was living on credit and trying to spend nothing. It was August of 2008 when I taught Edwene Gaines' book *The Four Spiritual Laws of Prosperity,* and sat down and read *Is Tithing For Me? By David Friedman* which served as a vivid remembering tools that allowed me to exit my state of financial fear. I immediately sat down and sent my regular tithes, and everything subsequently changed rather rapidly. I listed and sold the condo in less than three weeks. I moved back into the house and my son came to live with me for three years, which would not have been possible if I had been living in the loft condo that I purchased.

When my former husband and I started to attend Unity of Fayetteville back in 1987 we were tippers. We thought we were doing good to put $25 in the offering bag on Sunday morning. We thought of it in a similar way to paying a cover charge or for tickets to a musical or theater event. After we had attended for several months Rev. Gary Simmons, my first minister, gave a talk on tithing and we were shocked. He spoke about giving ten percent to the church. Mentioning money in our sparse visits to church before was a way to have the Hoskins family leave not ever to return. We thought that churches were "always asking for money". However, we loved going to Gary's "baby church" and did not want to stop attending. He mentioned a story of how he began to tithe in his first Unity church. He married a girl that already attended Unity and who tithed. She said that she would tithe on her income and he could begin tithing by giving one percent to the church.

When Rev. Gary (who wasn't Rev. Gary at the time) found that he did not miss the money, and that he was receiving so much benefit from the experience of attending the spiritual community's meeting, he could then increase it to two percent, and so on, and so on, until he reached ten percent. As we listened to that story we took a deep breath and began to give one percent. I hear folks all the time say that if they just earned more than they would give more. Having started at an engineering manager's salary, let me tell you it is just as hard to do on a larger salary as it is to tithe on a much smaller salary. It's why we talk about percentage giving. 1% of a lot is just as hard to give as is 1% of a little. It takes a shift in consciousness to do percentage giving at all, and as you will hear in the following story, having more does not make it easier. Please read this story and know that the essence of the story is repeated all over Unity, over and over again.

What I am offering in this class is an opportunity to feel your way into percentage giving. Allow your consciousness to take you to the next step, then the next, the next, and the next. The discipline of commitment and percentage giving has no upper limit. In the first chapter Butterworth gives an example of William Colgate. There is also Lord & Taylor. Some of you may remember the upscale department store, founded in 1826 in Manhattan by Mr. Taylor. You may ask when Mr. Lord joined the business. Mr. Taylor made the Lord his partner and put him first in all things, and hence Lord & Taylor. We are told that he eventually tithed fifty percent of the business, thereby putting God first in everything. Sharing with his "business partner" 50% as you would in any physical partnership. He unsurprisingly prospered beyond measure.

No matter what has been going on in my life at any given moment, positive or challenging, I have not forgotten the lessons inherent in fear, faith, lack, and choosing to give. I want to share David Friedman's article with you, and I would like you to read percentage generous giving when you read his word tithing. Learning generous percentage giving and how it will increase abundance in your life is part of David's story. Enjoy! Used with David's permission.

Is Tithing For Me?
By David Friedman

Of all the subjects discussed in Unity, tithing is perhaps the most controversial and misunderstood. Although it is universally touted by minister, teachers and students throughout the movement as the quickest and surest way to prosperity and peace, the idea of tithing, for many people, is surrounded by guilt, doubt, magical thinking and most of all fear.

One of the earmarks of Unity is that we consider ourselves to be students of the Truth. We do not, therefore, function on the basis of dogma or hearsay, rules and regulations or a literal interpretation of the Bible, but rather on the basis of what we can prove through thought, logic, personal experience and demonstration.

Tithing was a new concept to me when I arrived at Unity in 2002, so naturally I approached it with a great deal of suspicion. Was there a God, some guy up there, who was watching me, seeing how much I gave and giving it back to me multiplied? I doubted that. Was this a ploy by the church to make me feel guilty and give 'them' my money? Maybe. Was this absolute baloney, falling into the same woo-woo category as spells, magic, and superstition? Perhaps.

Since I was getting a lot out of being at Unity, and since tithing was one of the basic principles espoused by the movement. I decided that I needed to personally explore it for myself, and find some answers that I could trust and believe in. The first step was to get a clear definition of what tithing is.

Tithing-A Definition

The best definition of tithing that I have heard is the one given by Edwene Gaines in her prosperity workshops.

According to Edwene, tithing is giving 10% of all you receive back to the source of your spiritual food. It's not the same as giving a charitable contribution to someone in need. Charity is a good thing but it's not tithing. Tithing is not giving the 10% directly back to the person or place from which you physically receive it – you don't give it back to the person, job or organization that gave it to you, but rather to your spiritual source. Your spiritual source can be your church, a person who has given you spiritual food, a place that has given you spiritual food. Your whole tithe does not have to go to the same place, but may be divided among several people and places, as long as those people and places have been the source of your spiritual food.

Does Tithing Work For Me?

Now that I had a clear definition of what tithing is, my next logical question was, 'Does tithing work?" In order to find that out I signed up for a 4T class. 4T is a twelve-week curriculum in which you make an agreement to tithe to the church at which you're taking the course, a full 10% of all the money that comes in to you during that twelve weeks. The interesting thing about 4T is that you sign a paper guaranteeing that if, after the twelve weeks, you're not satisfied with the results, the church will give you back your tithe, no questions asked. So this was a no-risk situation.

The first week, I made $666. Very reluctantly, and with some measure of fear and irritation, I wrote a check for $66. I didn't like the idea of "throwing away" $66, but that was the agreement, so I did it.

The second week I earned $31,650! Horrified I wrote out a check for $3,165! Yikes! How could I be giving away that gigantic amount of money?

The third week I earned $21,400. Shaking and a bit irritated, I wrote another huge check.

This went on week after of week. You have to understand that I didn't as a rule, always earn that kind of money. But old royalty checks, new jobs, writing assignments kept pouring in from surprising places.

Around the tenth week, as I was writing yet another huge check, I suddenly stopped and thought; "This is so infuriating! Just when I start this class and agree to give away 10% of my income I start getting all these huge checks and have to give so much away. If I had taken this class three months ago I could have had to pay hardly anything! and then I got it. Ah, perhaps, just perhaps, tithing had something to do with it.

Now I'm aware that everyone's experience in the class was not the same, and some people tithe and tithe and nothing seems to happen. But for me, this was an actual experience where I had *tried tithing and something **had** happened. So my next question, naturally was, "Why?" Why and how does tithing work? Why did it work for me, and perhaps not for someone else? What was BEHIND it?*

Being a Truth student, and unwilling to be a wisher and hoper or a participant in magical thinking I set out to explore exactly what happens, in a nuts and bolts way, when we tithe.

How Tithing Works

If you owned a house with three other people, you wouldn't dream of not paying your share of the expenses every month. The house provides you with a home and with shelter, and by paying 1/4 of the mortgage and expenses, what you get is a home and shelter. You are causing that by paying your share. If you didn't pay your share you wouldn't have a home and shelter. Although you might not be happy about shelling out the money every month, or you might be fearful about how you were going to continue to get the money, every time you shell out the money, you get what you pay for, home and shelter. Were you to shell out more money, you could make your home fancier, or have some extra features that you wanted, or have a larger home. But at any rate, there is a direct, predictable correlation between what you give to the home and what you get from it. This is how it works on the physical plane.

You want a car that gives you transportation, which of course leads to other things like enjoyment, increased ability to have a livelihood, safety, peace of mind, whatever. So you pay the sticker price and you get the car. If you want a car that has a fabulous stereo system or better air conditioning or more room or more power or more safety features, you can pay more and you can get those things. Again, there is a direct correlation between what you pay and what you get for it. This is how it works on the physical plane.

So, the question is, "When you tithe to the source of spiritual food, what is it that you're paying for and what is it that you're getting?'

What You Are Paying For When You Tithe

When you receive something that is of value to you, you naturally want to keep it going. So the question is, "When you tithe to the source of your spiritual food, what do you receive back?"

Well first, let's look at what you receive from your source of spiritual food. Let's start with the church. Among the things that I receive from the church are:

A place to go every Sunday to be with people, to be with my inner and higher self, to be in prayer.

Camaraderie.

A place to meet people I might want to meet.

A place where I can contribute my talents, be they singing, writing, teaching, cooking, and where those talents are recognized and appreciated.

A place where I get spiritual guidance.

A place where I bring my problems, hear the minister, hear people's prayers, read things that help me to find ways through those issues.

In other words, a place where I receive NEW THOUGHTS.

A place where I find likeminded people who seem to understand what I'm talking about and support me in my feelings, whether I view those feelings as good or bad.

A place where I can take classes in things that interest me.

A place where I can offer classes in things that interest me.

A place where I can feel seen and important.

A place where I have personal access to business people, professionals, advisors who, outside of that context, might not be readily accessible to me.

A place where I can ask for what I want and be heard.

A place that is there to support me in manifesting my prosperity and my goals.

So when I looked at this list, I could see that the benefits I receive from the church basically fall into two categories, nuts and bolts physical-universe benefits, and spiritual benefits.

The nuts and bolts physical-universe category is the one in which it's easier to readily see what the benefits are. I can meet people, get information, study, learn, and find people with interests that match mine, use my talents, and get recognized for them, perhaps even profit financially from doing so. So, were I to contribute to the church and expand the church, what I would most likely get is more people to know, more classes to take, more chances to use my talents, more opportunity to get information and get close to people who might be helpful to me.

The less obvious, but perhaps most important benefits, are those we cannot see…the spiritual benefits. In order to assess those, we first have to explore what function spirit plays in our lives.

When we think about what we want in life, most of us start with the material, visible things: success, money, a great house (or two or three), a wonderful relationship, health—tangible things we can see, touch, taste and feel. Usually we are trained to go directly toward them by working harder, pushing, setting goals, trying, being ambitious, and working harder, pushing, setting goals, trying, being ambitious, and activities like that. For most of us, those activities work for a while, but then, as life goes on, we discover that we're trapped in certain cycles, the same things continue to fail for us, over and over we find ourselves constantly sabotaging ourselves or falling short of our goals. Or even worse, we achieve our goals and find, to our dismay, that we're not happy.

At some point, we begin to ask the question. "What is the real source of our happiness? In fact, what is the real cause of not only happiness but of the appearance of the things we want to have in our lives? We begin to ask the bigger questions like; "Why am I here? Why am I doing what I'm doing? What is it I'm really after?"

In response to these questions, and to the frustration of not having been able to get what we want through the means we've been trying, we come to an exploration of spirit. Is there something invisible, something in the realm of thought and feeling and soul and idea that is actually what is behind the realization of our dreams?

The basic question that is often asked in Unity is, "Are we physical beings have a spiritual life, or are we spiritual beings having a physical life?" This leads us to the more basic question of "Where does life really take place? In the things we can see outwardly, or in the invisible?"

Thought as Cause

In order to explore this question more fully for myself, I took on the leadership of the Artist's Group at Unity of New York in 2004. This was a group of artists that got together to support each other and to affirm their success and prosperity. Every week they would go around the room, and affirm things like "I am a wealthy, successful artist who is beloved by millions of people," and would think to myself, "No, you're not. You're just wishing you were."

This got me to thinking, "When we're affirming, what are we actually doing? Are we wishing and hoping, or are we affirming a truth?" Being only interested in the truth, I asked the question, "What in the spiritual world do I KNOW, without a doubt to be true?"

One thing that seems obvious to me is that everything is already given, already created, some of it is just visible and some of it isn't. When I write a song, I don't create it. I go into the infinite possibility of combinations of notes and words, put the ones I want together, and by putting them down on paper and singing them, bring them into manifestation, into visibility. But I didn't create that combination. It, and every other combination, was already there, in what I would call the Great Un-Manifested. When my song is finished being sung, it once again goes back into the Great Un-Manifested—it does not exist in the material, visible world until someone else sings it.

Bernoulli's principle of how a plane flies existed in the time of dinosaurs. Bernoulli didn't make it up, he just revealed it. Penicillin always had the power to kill bacteria, we just didn't know it until we revealed it. But it was always there. So the cures for every disease have already been created, we just haven't revealed some of them. Can you see that everything we could ever want, and ever not want, already exists? The question is just, "How do we reveal the things we want to reveal (or don't want to reveal for that matter?)"

The question, stated another way, is, "What is the relationship between things spiritual and things physical? What is the bridge that turns thought to manifestation, that turns idea into physical reality?"

To further explore this question for myself, I made a list of the things, non-visible, and visible, that I thought were contained in every life situation. There were THOUGHT, FEELING, BELIEF, and MANIFESTATION, three things in the non-physical, one in the physical. I looked at the things on this list, and set out to examine their relationship to one another.

I decided to start with feeling. The first thing I noticed was that I have never been able to change a feeling by going at it directly. I have never been able to say, "I won't feel angry. I'll feel peaceful, I won't feel sad, I'll feel happy, I won't feel jealous, I'll feel happily supportive." Although many of us have spent our lives trying to say "I don't feel this way or that way," in truth a feeling is a feeling is a feeling. However, I have noticed that when I change the thought behind a feeling, the feeling changes. So, for instance, if I'm feeling angry at someone, and some explanation or new fact comes into the picture, my feeling of anger will suddenly disappear. If I'm feeling frightened of something, a new piece of information about that thing can immediately change the fear. So if thought has the ability to generate and alter feeling, then we can say for the purpose of this exploration, that thought is "cause" and feeling is "effect" or result."

Next I thought, "Where does belief come from?" In looking at it, I realized that belief seems to be generated by a combination of thought and feeling. I feel a certain way, and when I think and feel this way, I believe that that's the way things are. For instance, I have the thought that I can't have something, out of that thought comes a feeling of fear, frustration and disappointment, and out of the combination of the two, I believe that it's a fact that it's not possible to have this. So a belief is a thought that we think is true.

One of the most frustrating things for me has been when someone says, "You've got to believe" something. Well, sorry, I either believe it or I don't, but I've never been able to change a belief. I've never been able to believe that I can when I believe that I can't. I've never been able to believe that something will happen when I believe it won't, unless I choose a new thought to think about it, which generates new feelings, the combination of which can generate new belief. So, belief could be thought of as an "effect" or "result" of thinking and feeling combined.

If we follow this further, we see that out of thinking, feeling and belief comes event or manifestation. We think something, feelings are generated, beliefs are generated, and lo and behold that's what shows up in our lives. Sometimes it's as a result of actions we've taken based on our thoughts, feelings and beliefs; sometimes it seems to just show up from nowhere, or from "outside" of us. But at any rate, based on the evidence we have before us, it could be said that what we see in our lives is merely a mirror of what we are thinking, feeling and believing.

Now the word "mirror" is very important. If you stand in front of a mirror and really look, you will observe several very interesting things. First of all, a mirror is the only way you can see what your face looks like. Think about that for a minute. You can NEVER see your face—you could *have a huge scar on it, it could be what you call attractive or ugly, it could be dirty or clean and you wouldn't even know. You have no idea what you look like. You must have the mirror to see it. But, and this is very important, the mirror is not you. It looks EXACTLY like you but there is really nothing there. You'd have to be nuts to see an outfit in the mirror and start trying to change it by reaching into the mirror. That could NEVER work because what you're seeing in the mirror isn't there. It's only a **reflection** of reality.*

The other obvious feature about a mirror is that it always reflects exactly what's in front of it, at exactly the moment that it's in front of it, in the exact way in which it's in front of it. You don't move your hand and a couple of seconds later the mirror moves. So if manifestation is a direct reflection of thought, feeling and belief, it doesn't have a time lag. You don't believe something for a while and then it shows up. The mirror or manifestation is reflecting EXACTLY what you're thinking and feeling and believing RIGHT NOW. It doesn't catch up, it doesn't take time, it's your thoughts, feelings and beliefs that are taking the time or changing gradually.

So what we've got in this model, is THOUGHT causes FEELING, the combination of these two lead to BELIEF, and the combination of these two lead to MANIFESTATION or what we see in the "mirror" of life. Feeling, Belief and Manifestation therefore, cannot be chosen or altered by going directly at them, since they are not their own cause but rather are ultimately caused by thought. So the question becomes, "Can we choose our thoughts?"

Most often, people choose their thoughts based on what they've just seen manifested, living in the illusion that the physical world causes their thoughts. That would be like saying that your image in the mirror is the cause of the way you look.

When I look at the notion of thought, I realize that every thought already exists, and we have the capability of thinking any thought we like. I didn't say we have to feel it. I didn't say we have to believe it. It's very important that one make that distinction. But it is possible for me right now, to simply think the thought, "I am good looking." It is equally possible for me to think the thought, "I am ugly". What effect would walking around thinking one or the other of those thoughts have on my life? What choices would I make? Where would I go? What would I try and not try? Who would I ask out? What would people's response to me be? How would my life end up looking if I went through it always having the thought "I am ugly"? How would it look if I went through it with the thought "I am good looking"? What, after repeatedly thinking this thought, might I come to feel? What might I come to believe? And what might come to be in the physical reality around me?

So What Does All This Have to Do With Tithing

What I discovered, through this exploration into thought, feeling, belief and manifestation, is that tithing, being an action in the physical realm, is not a cause of prosperity, but rather is an effect of prosperity thinking. If that is the case, it would follow that prosperity thinking must already be in place for a person to even be able to be willing to take the action of tithing. In other words, prosperity thinking precedes tithing.

There's an important shift that has to happen for someone to become a person who tithes. Some people make this shift unconsciously, some have to come to it consciously, but however it occurs, it's a result of a change in their thinking. In order to tithe, one must shift from thinking that the world is a physical place, to the understanding that the world is a spiritual place. Another way of saying this is that one must shift from thinking of the actions and events of the world as the cause of not only other action and events, but as the cause of thought and spirit, to knowing that it is thought that causes action and events.

The act of tithing represents a knowing that there is unlimited abundance, that whatever you give comes back to you, and that you don't have to worry about money or cling to it or be run by it. Would that be a wonderful thing to know? Well that's what a person has to know in order to even be able to tithe. So when you contemplate tithing, if you're having trouble doing it, what you're really having trouble with is taking on the thought that abundance, money and prosperity are flowing freely in the universe, exist in infinite amounts, are there for the taking by anyone who cares to reveal them, and do not need to be worried about. You think you're tithing so that you can find that out, but actually you have to already have taken on that thought in order to be tithing in the first place. So tithing is the evidence that you already have that thought, not the cause of it.

Since, as we discussed above, thought can be freely chosen, the resistance to tithing is actually our resistance to having the thought of abundance. And if we subscribe to the principles discussed above, acknowledging that thought is cause, then we cannot see abundance until we have the thought of abundance.

So one could say, "Why not just have the thought? Why tithe?" Well my experience has been that tithing is the natural result of that thought. The only way we can see that thought, entertain it and live it is in the mirror of the world. So the fun of that thought is seeing it in action, working it, knowing it works. What would be the fun of having a beautiful outfit on, if you never got to see it? Or never showed it to anyone? Or never got to see the response of the world to it? Isn't it fun to see it? Doesn't it then encourage you to know more about what looks good on you, to feel more confident, to have more beautiful clothes?

So ultimately, church is a source of Thought. The spiritual food we get from church is the New Thought, the thought that makes things appear in our lives as a reflection of itself. So the more we feed that thought, the more it appears both in our minds and in the physical "mirror" before us, and it becomes an endless circle of growth and prosperity. By tithing, we are increasing and keeping alive the place from which that thought arises (the church, our friends, whatever our conduit of spiritual food is), and it is that thought, not work or manipulation or pushing or notoriety, that appears in the world as everything we could want to see in the world.

So to use the circle we spoke of before, here are two charts showing how tithing and not tithing would look from the perspective of thought as cause

THOUGHT

The more I give, the more I get.
Abundance naturally flows to me.
I can't out give God.

TITHING

MANIFESTATION

(Mirror of the thought, feeling,
and belief)
I TITHE
(I give it away freely)
Prosperity flows to me
All that I desire and more
Appears effortlessly

FEELING

Confidence
Peace
Safety
Abundance

BELIEF

Everything I want and need is
easily and already here for me

THOUGHT

I have to hold onto money.
There is scarcity in the world.
Giving money is giving it away
and it won't come back.

NOT TITHING

MANIFESTATION

(Mirror of the thought, feeling,
and belief)
I hold onto my money.
Lack, scarcity, difficult,
poverty, etc....

FEELING

Fear
Scarcity
Suspicion
Sense of danger

BELIEF

You don't get back what you give.
There isn't enough to go around.
The world is not an abundant place.

You can see from these charts that the thoughts that lead naturally to tithing, the thoughts behind tithing, the thoughts that cause tithing, create a circle of ever increasing, easy abundance, while the thoughts that lead to not tithing create a circle of lack and fear.

Creating the World As You Want It to Be

The actions that come out of thoughts of prosperity and abundance allow you to create the world as you want it to be. The following is a story of charitable contribution rather than a story of tithing, but I think it makes the point well.

Each year at Christmas time, the post office receives thousands of letters from underprivileged kids who write to Santa. The letters are made available to the public so that people can take them and anonymously send the requested gifts to the kids.

One year, I picked up a lovely letter in which an eight-year-old girl spoke of how both her parents were out of work, but that she was still grateful that Santa existed, whether or not he brought her gifts. She went on to say how sad she felt for all the people lost in the World Trade Center, as well as all the people who lost people, and said she prayed for them every day. It was a truly touching and lovely letter. Then she went on to ask for a bear, some chapter books and a few computer items.

Touched by her compassion and her requests, I decided to go all out. I went to Toys 'R Us and bought a giant bear that was bigger than I am. I then bought a whole bunch of chapter books, and went to K-Mart and got a $300 gift certificate. I got a red piece of paper and headed it "SANTA CLAUS—North Pole," and wrote her a note, thanking her for her lovely letter, telling her that I hoped she liked the bear and the books, and explaining that she should have her mommy take her to K-Mart where she could exchange the gift certificate for exactly the things she wanted. I finished the letter by saying, "Remember, dreams can come true."

I sent it off anonymously, I was filled with a wonderful feeling. When I examined that feeling, I realized that it didn't come from the sense that I was so generous and so giving, but rather from a sense that I now lived in a world where someone could send an impossible wish out into the universe and get it filled by an unknown and unseen source in a way greater than they could ever imagine. And the reason I lived in that world was that I had created it. If I, as a regular person, could be the fulfiller of that dream, that meant that it was totally possible that I could have a wish or a dream that I thought was impossible , and someone I don't even know or some set of circumstances I wasn't even aware of could fulfill it beyond my wildest dreams. That was such a wonderful thought and feeling, created entirely by an action I'd taken based on the thought of the possibility of abundance. Can you see how I already had to have that thought in order to take that action, but the existence of the thought and the feeling and sense of security and possibility I got from it were only apparent to me after I had taken the action?

Tithing is an Exchange of Energy

When we understand that everything has already been created, is already here, then tithing, rather than giving to get something, becomes merely an exchange of energy. Let me give an example of what I mean.

When you buy a house, you are not actually giving away money to get something, but in fact are converting one asset (money) into another (a house). The house is worth as much as the money is, and in fact, in most cases a house will grow in value faster than money just sitting there will. So when you buy a million-dollar house, you are not giving away a million dollars and getting a thing, you are taking a million dollars and converting it to something else that is also worth a million dollars. There is nothing lost, just changed from cash (that is just cash and sits there and can do nothing in itself), to a house which can give you shelter and joy and also grow in value faster than the cash can.

So knowing that, it follows that one could constantly be trying to give as much as possible to the source of thoughts, since those thoughts will only bring about more abundance. This is why people who know this, people who have already taken on the thought that this is the way it works, often tithe way more than 10% of their income to their spiritual source.

Try It!

So the whole question of tithing rests on whether you believe that thought is the cause of abundance or vice versa. And the only way I know of to prove that to yourself is to try it. Every time I try it, it works for me. I get to create the world the way I want to see it.

I recommend that, with the knowledge you now have, you put tithing to the text. Choose the thought of unlimited abundance, out of that thought, give back at least 10% of all that comes into your source of spiritual food, watch that source grow and thrive and give you back more thoughts of abundance which allow you to take more abundant actions which allow you to receive more thoughts of abundance, and watch the circle grow richer and richer.

If you're not seeing results right away, don't look to those results. Look to your thoughts. Every time you notice a thought of non-abundance or fear, exchange it for a thought of unlimited abundance. Use the mirror of your life only to let yourself know what it is you're causing by thought. When you see something you don't want, don't take out the Windex and try to wipe the mirror. Instead go to the source—your thought—and exchange that. You will soon notice that the mere fact that you are tithing will be the physical world reflection of your unlimited thoughts of abundance.

It's a wonderful feeling to be the cause of such ever increasing abundance for yourself and for the whole world. Sort of like being God. In fact, exactly like being God. I suppose that's what we mean when we say we're made in God's image.

Happy tithing![xlvi]

An Integral Approach to:

Creating Sustainable Prosperity!

Chapter 11

Giving is More Than a Cash Donation

GIVING IS MORE THAN A CASH DONATION

Looking at giving must include much more than the checks that you write intentionally to give to the source of your spiritual good because we are not only dealing in the upper right quadrant where the mechanics of giving happen. We are also dealing in the upper left quadrant, which is the realm of Spirit, of energy, and of attitudes. Scripture says that, "Each of you should give what you have decided in your heart to give, not reluctantly, or under compulsion, for God loves a cheerful giver." II Corinthians 9:7. Now, this is not about obeying a dictate of the Bible. It is about observing and taking note of how the Universe works.

Because we are energy, and money is energy, the people and institutions that we give to are also energy, and therefore it is also about how the giver's energy touches the receiver's energy. I would like to remind you again that the desire to give must be a part of the gift you give every time money is exchanged. I invite you to also look at the energy you have when you pay what we call "bills." Are you acknowledging the gifts you have received in exchange for the money you are giving, the money you use to "pay your bills"; this includes looking at your values and how they are represented in each individual expenditure you make. Are you noticing and being grateful for the gift you have received in exchange for your money? For example, are you noticing what you value about your home when you pay your rent or mortgage? Are you being grateful for the fresh water, light, heat and cooling when you pay your utilities? Are you grateful for the ability to be mobile when you pay your automobile expenses? If you see each payment as representing a fulfillment of your desires and an expression of your values, no longer is it a burden to sit down and pay your bills. It becomes an opportunity to say thank you and be grateful. See if you can make each exchange of money be an expression of gratitude, and notice how this change affects your overall abundance.

Tipping is another way you express your generosity. If you have ever spent any time as a waiter or a waitress, a bartender, a stylist, or a parking attendant, then you very likely and intimately understand the concept. You are aware of the work that is done for each customer, and you can also see how each tip you give is how you give is an expression of your appreciation. Questions to consider, are you a "stingy" or a "generous" tipper? Can you see that how you tip may also represent how you receive the gifts that are given to you? The energy of the Universe reacts to all of the energy that we put out. You can simply notice, are you primarily a giver, or a receiver? Are you generous or are you out to get more than you give? All of this impacts your sustainable prosperity.

How about the folks that we frequently see with signs at highway off-ramps? It may not be about whether or not you "give" them anything but about how you react to the person themselves. Do you look at them? Do you smile at them acknowledging them as a person endowed with the same Divine Spirit that you have within you? Or do you look the other way, ignoring them? Are you looking for opportunities to "give" acknowledgment to other individuals? It can be one of our biggest giving opportunities. How about the individuals that mow your lawn, shovel your snow, clean your house or do your repairs? Do you compensate them as you want to be compensated for the work that you do, or are you always trying to pay the least amount possible to get the jobs done for you?

You may ask how else do I give? You give of your time. You give of your talents. You give with your gratitude. You give with every interaction that you have. How do you serve? When do you serve? Looking at all aspects of giving is important. Perhaps you can think of many ways that you give that I have not listed. It is about noticing and making your conscious choices based on the best information that you have at the moment.

HOW DO I DECIDE

This is a question that each of us has to uncover for ourselves. If this were any other tithing class you would have already, the first time the class met, made a commitment to tithe ten percent of your gross income for the duration of the class. As David Friedman says in his story above, "...tithing being an action in the physical realm, is not a cause of prosperity, but rather, is an effect of prosperity thinking, if that is the case it would follow that prosperity thinking must already be in place for a person to even be able to be willing to take the action of tithing. In other words, prosperity thinking precedes tithing." There is power in making the **commitment** to give a percentage of your income to the source or sources of your spiritual good. It changes the energy of your thinking and your feelings of abundance. At the same time, I want to encourage you to look at the reality of your Allocation of Money Sheet. Where is the discretionary income? How are you going to re-allocate that to accommodate the percentage of your income that you are now going to allocate to giving to the source of your spiritual good?

I continue to give ten percent and 20% when I tip, even though I no longer think of it "as the law"—but rather because math is not my strong suit, I can do ten percent pretty easily, seven or thirteen percent not as easily. I have not yet been able to see twenty percent in my discretionary income so that I can choose to give that amount. I chose the number twenty because I can do the math to double ten. Now, I know that all of you are not as math challenged as I am, and I also know that you all either own a calculator or have one on your phone. You will be able to figure it out and write the check, or have the correct number to fill in on your credit card donation sheet. I know that you and The Divine Within You, will know exactly the percentage that is right for you to begin with. I also invite you to hold the space that as your prosperity thinking increases, the percentage that you choose to give to the sources of your spiritual good will also increase. That is why I encourage you to do the sheets in pencil and to have a good eraser so that you can change the numbers as your experience changes.

Please look at David Friedman's diagram again. This time I have modified it just a little to reflect what I am suggesting to you. Another reminder to know that giving isn't just about money although that is an easy concrete place to see the law at work in your life. Giving is about what you want to receive in your Universe. God is present in all things or "May the Force be With You" as you prayerfully consider the percentage that you choose to give.

THOUGHT

The more I give, the more I get.

Abundance naturally flows to me.

I can't out give God.

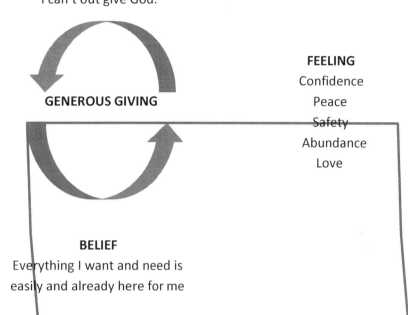

MANIFESTATION

(Mirror of the thought, feeling,

and belief)

I GIVE GENEROUSLY

(and I give it away freely)

Prosperity flows to me

All that I desire and more

Appears effortlessly

GENEROUS GIVING

FEELING

Confidence

Peace

Safety

Abundance

Love

BELIEF

Everything I want and need is

easily and already here for me

THIS IS IN ESSENCE A DIAGRAM OF THE LAW OF THE UNIVERSE.

WHAT WE GIVE OUT IS WHAT WE GET BACK. IF IT IS TOO HARD TO SEE IN YOUR OWN LIFE NOTICE IT

IN OTHERS AND THEN BE AWARE THAT IT IS HAPPENING IN YOUR LIFE AS WELL.

THIS LAW FALLS UNDER THE CATEGORY OF *SIMPLE… but not EASY.*

THOUGHT

I have to hold onto money.

There is scarcity in the world.

Giving money [ANYTHING] is giving it away

and it won't come back.

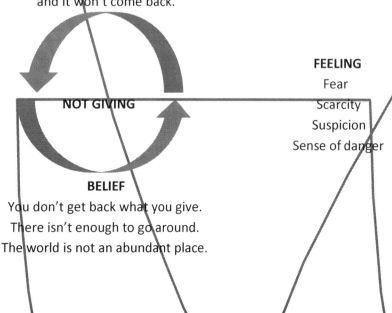

MANIFESTATION

(Mirror of the thought, feeling,

and belief)

I hold onto my money.

Lack, scarcity, difficult,

poverty, etc....

NOT GIVING

FEELING

Fear

Scarcity

Suspicion

Sense of danger

BELIEF

You don't get back what you give.

There isn't enough to go around.

The world is not an abundant place.

BASED ON *MY VALUES*

I,_____CHOOSE THE FOLLOWING WAYS TO ALLOCATE MY MONEY:

NAME

This is your worksheet. We will create a final version later. Do this in pencil and have your eraser handy.

My weekly Net Income: $_____

Look at your six weeks of cash purchases and average those amounts into a cash purchases per week, leaving out any extraordinary one-time expense that might have occurred. (May belong in categories below)

$_____

Now look at your discretionary and non-discretionary expenses over the last six weeks. List them by categories. There are some listed below. Feel free to add others or leave a category blank if it does not apply to you. Look at the value represented by each category. Notice if there is a category that you did not spend money on in the last six weeks that should be included, i.e. vacation. Be sure to include it now. Consult your desires and any financial requirements. Make sure that you have included them and the estimate of what they will require on a monthly basis.

VALUE	AMOUNT	
*My Generous Giving to the Source(s) of my Spiritual Good*_____%		_____
Auto	_____	
Fuel		_____
Insurance		_____
Loan		_____
Registration		_____
Service/Maintenance		_____
Business Expenses	_____	_____
Charity (Giving)	_____	_____
Clothing	_____	_____
Computer (Technology)	_____	_____
Education	_____	_____
Entertainment (Recreation)	_____	_____
Gifts Given	_____	_____
Groceries	_____	_____
Housing	_____	
HOA Fees		_____
Insurance		_____

Mortgage/Rent   _____

Mortgage Insurance   _____

Utilities

         Cable TV   _____

         Garbage & Recycling   _____

         Gas & Electric   _____

         Internet   _____

         Telephone(s)   _____

         Water   _____

Insurance   _____

         Disability   _____

         Life   _____

         Medical   _____

Interest Expense   _____   _____

IRA (Retirement Contribution   _____   _____

Medical   _____

         Doctors   _____

         Medicine   _____

Misc.   _____

Personal Care   _____   _____

Pets   _____   _____

Savings   _____   _____

Taxes   _____

         City   _____

         Federal   _____

         State   _____

         Medicare   _____

         SDI

         Social Security   _____

Vacation   _____   _____

         Total   _____

LOWER LEFT AND LOWER RIGHT QUADRANTS

I	IT
My Spiritual Experience of Abundance Spiritual Teachings About Prosperity Transcendent Inner World How "I AM" in Relation to the Experience of Money— Context and Feelings	Material and Outer World Banking, Checkbooks Salaries, Credit Cards Mortgages the IRS Facts, Time Management Budget New Worth Take Details of Money Seriously It's up to You to Use Your Gifts Seriously, You are the Owner
WE	**ITS**
All of the Communities We are a Part of How each Community Relates to Money The Community's Unique Context around an Organization's Finances	Your Community's Financial Details— Profit and Loss Sheets Budgets Net Worth You are the Owner of your Community Interdependence of Human Beings Taxes—What They Buy

Every page of work in this book that you have done for yourselves needs to be worked on an organization wide basis for every group that you are a part of if you care about their finances and the health of the organization. It is "your" church, "your" club, "your" neighborhood, "your" children's schools, and "your" city. You can as a group talk about each chapter and how it is relevant to your organization. When you are creating a budget for an organization that you care about you will again first look at the current fixed expenses. These are the expenses that happen whether you open the doors or not. Then you look at the expenses that you would like to have. This needs to be done by all of the leaders, or elected leaders of the organization. In order to finish the work effectively it is important to call the leadership, and membership if possible, to affirm the desires of the group. It is important that the expenses are estimated as accurately and precisely as possible. Even having a range would be good, a high end, and a more economical version. Once you have some good numbers it is up to the individuals in the room (the leadership first, and the community second) to commit to what portion of the expenses they as individual contributors can be counted on to supply. It is much like a family's budget. Everyone may want to go on a cruise, ski in Vail, or go on that trip to Disney World. However, when the money is added up, that everyone is willing to give, and it does not match all of the potential desires that exist, given the finances that will be available, firm decisions must be made by those same decision makers. It is the commitment and buy-in that matter in the final decisions for organizations. Just as an individual family would take advantage of extra income that is available, so can an organization, but knowing that the core requirements will be met is a sound way for an organization to make good financial decisions.

In Unity churches, in particular, this method of operation is not how financial decisions have been made in most of the churches in which I have been a part. We have usually and simply "trusted" that the money that we needed would be forthcoming. Sometimes that trust has been justified. Often it has resulted in financial shortfalls and frustration because "they" or "so and so" have not supported the church enough. If we start with a plan, put numbers to the plan, get commitments to carry out that plan, AND trust the Universe as we continue to work the guidelines outlined in this book, as applied to organizations, I believe that Unity churches and our national and international organizations will also thrive. We must move from the lower left quadrant of our faith, to also encompassing the facts of the lower right-hand quadrant to have financially stable churches or other institutions.

I know some are asking if this is really possible. I would like to say that the start-up church that I currently serve has demonstrated this beautifully. At the beginning of their second summer the church's finances were in negative territory. Since we were a new organization the question that had to be answered by the people who made up the organization was firstly, do you want to be a church? I asked them to discuss and answer this question without my presence in the room. I did this because they were the ones that have to make the church work.

When they answered in the affirmative then the people around the table had to make commitments as to their own giving. When the number did not match the current budget they were the ones that decided what they were going to fund and what they were going to do without until the amount of money increased beyond the minimum level. They made those hard choices. They then lived with the result of their decision. They actually increased the amount that they were paying me and decreased the number of musicians that we hired each Sunday. I am not sure I would have made the decision that they made. However, I was willing to support their choices. Those commitments have been honored and the number of musicians has been increased as the giving increased. They made the decisions based on their values. I believe that is an integral way to make financial decisions for an organization. There was no perfect agreement in the discussions but there was perfect alignment once the decision was made. In some organizations they would call that "pledging". The word was never used by this group, the results were the same, and it has continued to work in the present.

Also, I am guessing that each of you reading and working this book live in the United States. I am also very confident that as citizens and inhabitants of the United States you also live in a state, county, and a city or township. I can also say with absolute confidence that if you are reading this book you are also a citizen of the earth. What this means to me is that the town or city, county, state, and country are all mine, yours, and our responsibility, collectively.

We most likely all take advantage of the public infrastructure, like public schools, roads, bridges, and various social services from time to time. Personally, I take advantage of Social Security and Medicare. Additionally, the fire department comes when I call and the library is available to lend me books, DVD's, CD's, and more. They can only do this based on the funds that we have given them over the course of our lives through public revenues. We call these funds taxes. I have no desire to cheat on my taxes, take money under the table, or in any other way minimize my tax obligation in an unlawful way. Now, I do take advantage of the tax breaks that are offered to me legally, through deductions, credits, and exemptions. However, once again, we are talking about the energy with which this money is given and received, and the integrity we use in determining how much our obligation is, must always be taken into consideration. If we value having freedom, schools, roads, and all of the services provided to us by our government then we need to express our gratitude with the money we give them...called taxes.

We are energetic wholes—brought together and interwoven through a metaphysical fabric that permeates everything in the universe. There are no parts of our lives that are excluded from this energy exchange. We cannot cross our fingers and wish; we cannot hope that the money we receive will not be noticed or taxed accordingly. It's not just about whether we will be audited. It's about our own integrity with the Universe, even exchange. My Quicken program has a category called "Income Other." I have even copied $100 bills when I have been paid for a wedding or a funeral in cash, and I then add that to my W-4 statement so that my tax obligations include the total amount that I have been paid.

You may think I'm crazy. However, I feel good that I am supporting the country, state and city that I value. Several years ago the Manse Laws for ministers changed and I was inattentive to that change. As a result of that and my withdrawing money from my IRA, and having to also pay tax on that amount, I ended up with an income tax liability of $11,000, in addition to what I had paid in that year. At that time, I did not have $11,000 to pay that liability. I found out that the IRS allows us to make installment payments to pay our annual tax obligations, and I have been paying that amount down at $400 a month, an amount that I felt I could handle. By the time you read this I will have paid that amount off. I believe that friends, family, and acquaintances will verify that I have never once complained, nor have I tried to get out of paying that obligation.

I believe that sustainable prosperity requires that level of integrity in all of our dealings with money and the energy that money represents.

An Integral Approach to:

Creating Sustainable Prosperity!

Chapter 12

Conclusion

CONCLUSION

Remember that we are doing this work as an extension of Unity's 5th Principle. Stated in my own words, the 5th principle says, "It's not enough to know the truth, we must live the truth that we know." For me this principle also implies the African Proverb about not giving fish to people but teaching them to fish. This book is about teaching the components of sustainable prosperity. Not teaching it just for "miracles" to happen, not just teaching it to help balance the church budget, but teaching it so that the skills involved serve each person taking the course for the rest of their lives.

This is a start, a beginning to attempt to integrate the different aspects of our financial lives by utilizing the teachings of money, wealth, and abundance that have been taught for over a hundred years. We then combine that teaching with the practical aspects of money that are even older. As we integrate our spiritual and financial lives we are taking additional steps to the wholeness and awareness that we seek.

Making conscious choices on the when, where, and what you spend money on is of paramount concern, which includes being aware of the energy of money itself and the context within which we live our monetary lives. Knowing what we value and spending our money according to those values are all part of living life effectively. Allocating our money properly so that the money is there to pay the annual or semi-annual bills that we have should take precedence. We should not be scrambling because there is an unfunded bill that is staring us in the face that cannot be successfully addressed on time.

By recognizing that desire is an important part of our lives, by being aware of our desires, and by making action plans and being aware of the financial requirements to make them happen, again, leads to wholeness and our ability to live empowered and fulfilled lives. Noticing when a desire has been fulfilled and noting those successes brings more gratitude into our lives.

Be aware of the spiritual component of money. Knowing that money is an essential part of our lives and realizing that we are channels for the abundance of the Universe when we are filled with knowing that it is so. In reality the only thing that ever blocks our abundance is our own fear, any sense of unworthiness, and any lack of forgiveness that we might harbor towards any person, organization, or institution that we believe has wronged us at some point in the past. These are all the parts of this book. There is more information available if you need more work in any particular area. Please see the bibliography, in addition to financial advice that is typically taught in classes and by financial planners.

I have said almost nothing about the work of Ken Wilber, whose work is the basis of this course. It is his approach to all of the information that exists that has broadened my view of prosperity and abundance. Talking about Wilber briefly is not one of the things that lends itself to simple explanations, to put it mildly. One of the simplistic ways that I talk about it is that "nobody is ever 100 percent wrong or 100 percent right. It is a matter of checking the information to see which quadrant it belongs in. When we understand the viewpoint being presented we know how to respond to the information.

Information in the left hand quadrants, either "I" or "WE," is experiential. It cannot really be quantified because it is either my experience or it is our experience. However, the world is incomplete without the information of the right-hand quadrants, which is totally quantifiable. Both are correct, yet only true when rightly combined and understood. Wilber talks about AQUAL, all quadrants, all levels, and all lines. I have used only the most basic of his premises in this book. Studying and understanding Wilber is the work of a lifetime, and not all of you will be inspired to delve into his work. It is abundant online and a simple book to start with is *The Integral Vision: A Very Short Introduction to the Revolutionary Integral Approach to Life, God, the Universe, and Everything*. That is the scope of his work and life study.

I would again like to express my gratitude to the following: Rev. Jill Andrews, Suzanne Scott, Nancy Smith, Alicia Slagle, and Toni Vodnik for being willing to work with the drafts of this material and help me turn it into a real and usable book. It has been quite the joyous experience to write, and it is my sincerest hope that it is useful and interesting to you, your family, your friends, and your spiritual community, and that it furthers your journey towards sustainable prosperity.

APPENDIX

THE TWELVE STEPS

AA Step 1

"We admitted we were powerless over alcohol and that our lives had become unmanageable."
The first step of AA is to admit that you have a problem. Those who are not ready to admit to a problem may not be able to seek the help they need, and they may be more likely to return to drinking. Accepting that a problem exists and facing it may be difficult, but it makes the person aware of it. Admitting it to other people enforces the issue.

AA Step 2

"Came to believe that a power greater than ourselves could restore us to sanity."
Many programs focus on participants having hope and faith that they will return to a healthy state. These programs may involve God, spirituality and meditation in the healing process. Not all programs focus on religion, however.

AA Step 3

"Made a decision to turn our will and our lives over to the care of God as we understood Him."
AA is not strictly a Christian organization. Different groups work with different types of spirituality and religions, and choosing the right one can help participants feel more comfortable and accepted.

AA Step 4

"Made a searching and fearless moral inventory of ourselves."
A major step that happens after admitting a problem is admitting to your faults. Each participant in the program has to look at his past and present situations and determine any faults that he has. By admitting to these problems, the group and the individual can try to fix them.

AA Step 5

"Admitted to God, to ourselves and to another human being the exact nature of our wrongs."
Knowing what you have done wrong and admitting it are two very different things. Admitting past errors and wrongs to a group and receiving support to change your life is a part of AA that all participants go through.

AA Step 6

"Were entirely ready to have God remove all these defects of character."
Once you've admitted all the problems and faults of character, it is time to let go and accept that it is time to change. Accepting responsibility for the change is part of this step.

AA Step 7

"Humbly asked Him to remove our shortcomings."
Since a major part of most AA groups is spirituality, this step focuses on healing, prayer, meditation, hope and faith.

AA Step 8

"Made a list of all persons we had harmed and became willing to make amends to them all."
Sometimes, people come to AA thinking there is no way back from their current situations. But, that isn't always

the case. By making a list of all the people harmed by the alcoholism and being willing to try to make amends, a participant is accepting responsibility and understanding what has been wrong in his life. This step is more about the planning and acceptance of making amends rather than completing the task.

AA Step 9

"Made direct amends to such people wherever possible, except when to do so would injure them or others." In many cases, admitting you're wrong, apologizing and informing a person that you're getting help is enough to have that person's support. However, sometimes people have been seriously hurt or are in a position where an apology or trying to make amends would make a situation worse. Through the group, decisions can be made as to who will be best served by trying to make amends and who may be more hurt by it than anything else. For instance, drunk driving accidents may be something a person wants to apologize for, but not all people will be ready to hear an apology.

AA Step 10

"Continued to take personal inventory and when we were wrong, promptly admitted it."
A major part of the program is continuing to take responsibility for your actions. If you fall back into drinking, it's important to stop and admit it. Relapses are normal, and the group can be supportive while you're healing. Admitting trouble with quitting, or trouble with other parts of your life, are not signs of weakness. It is meant to help keep participants on track to a healthier lifestyle.

AA Step 11

"Sought through prayer and meditation to improve our conscious contact with God as we understood Him, praying only for knowledge of His will for us and he power to carry that out."
Whether or not a person is religious, this allows him to have quiet time where he can reflect on the day, what has happened recently and the things he needs to do to make his life better.

AA Step 12

"Having had a spiritual awakening as the result of these steps, we tried to carry this message to alcoholics and to practice these principles in all our affairs." Another serious aspect of the 12-step program is giving back to the community that has helped you to receive the treatment you needed. The main point of this is to help others seek help when they need it and sometimes to give a person someone else to feel responsible for, as this can help them focus on more positive aspects of life. Community service, aiding others and working with future AA groups are all normal choices for this step.

The 12-step program has been successful for many people, and it can be successful for you or a loved one as well. If you would like more information on a 12-step program near you, call us at 1-888-249-7292. We are available to talk to you about your options 24 hours a day, seven days a week.

Bibliography

Adyashanti (2011). *Falling into grace: insights on the end of suffering.* Sounds True, Boulder, Colorado.

Breathnach, Sarah Ban (1995). *Simple abundance: a daybook of comfort and joy.* Warner Books, New York, NY.

Brumet, Robert (2013). *Living originally: ten spiritual practices to transform your life.* Unity Books, Unity Village.

Butterworth, Eric (1998). *Spiritual economics: the principles and process of true prosperity.* Unity House. Unity Village.

Cady, H. Emilie. *Lessons in truth.* Unity Books, Unity Village.

Charles Fillmore Reference Library (1959). *The revealing word.* Twelfth printing 1994. Unity Books, Unity Village.

Fillmore, Charles (1936). *Prosperity.* Unity Books, Unity Village.

Friedman, David. (2005). *Is tithing for me? a practical exploration of tithing.* Middler Music Publishing, Inc. Norwalk, CT.

Gaines, Edwene Gaines (2005). *The four spiritual laws of prosperity: a simple guide to unlimited abundance.* Rodale. Distributed by Holtzbrinck Publishers.

Gibran, Khalil, *The prophet.*

Keyes, Ken Jr. (1986 twenty-first printing). *Handbook to Higher Consciousness.* Living Love Center, Coos Bay, OR.

McTaggart, Lynne (2007). The intention experiment: using your thoughts to change your life and the world. Free Press, a Division of Simon & Schuster, Inc., New York, NY.

Needleman, Jacob (1991). *Money and the meaning of life.* Doubleday, New York.

Nemeth, Maria (1997). *You and money: would it be all right with you if life got easier?* Vildehiya Publications, Sacramento, CA.

Orman, Suze. 1997. *The 9 steps to financial freedom.* Crown Publishers, Inc. New York.

Sinetar, Marcia, (1987). *Do What You Love the Money Will Follow: discovering your right livelihood.* Dell Publishing NY, NY.

Wattles, Wallace D. (1910) (2007), *The science of getting rich: the proven mental program to a life of wealth.* The Penguin Group, NY, NY.

Wigglesworth, Cindy. 2012. *SQ21: the twenty-one skills of spiritual intelligence.* Select Books, Inc. New York

Wilber, Ken. (2007) *The Integral vision: a very short introduction to the revolutionary integral approach to life, god, the universe, and everything. Shambhala, Boston, MA.*

any of Wilber's books on Integral Theory and his web sites:

http://www.kenwilber.com/home/landing/index.html

http://integrallife.com/contributors/ken-wilber

http://www.merriam-webster.com/concise/tithe?show=0&t=1361235558

References

Chapter 1

Butterworth, Eric (1998). *Spiritual economics: the principles and process of true prosperity*. Unity House. Unity Village.

Chapter 2

[i] Fillmore, C. (1959), (1994). *Revealing word,* Unity Books, Unity Village, MO. 135.
[ii] Needleman, Jacob. (1994). *Money and the meaning of life.* Doubleday, NY, NY. 3.
[iii] Ibid., 118.
[iv] Ibid., 175.
[v] Ibid., 182.
[vi] Ibid., 3.
[vii] Ibid., 6.
[viii] Ibid., 6.

[ix] Nemeth, Maria (1997). *You and money: would it be all right with you if life got easier?* Vildehiya Publications, Sacramento, CA. 15.

[x] Ibid. 14.

Chapter 3

[xii] Needleman, Jacob (1991). *Money and the meaning of life*. Doubleday, New York. 77.

[xiii] Ibid. 87.
[xiv] Ibid. xi.
[xv] Ibid. xvii.
[xvi] Ibid. 2,3.
[xvii] Ibid. 41.
[xviii] Ibid. 41.
[xix] Ibid. 59.
[xx] Ibid. 103.
[xxi] Ibid. 109.
[xxii] Ibid. 113.
[xxiii] Ibid. 124.
[xxiv] Ibid. 126.
[xxv] Ibid. 133.
[xxvi] Ibid. 161.

Chapter 4

[xxvii] Fillmore, Charles (1936). *Prosperity*. Unity Books, Unity Village. 173.

[xxviii] Cady, H. Emilie. *Lessons in truth*. Unity Books, Unity Village. 67,68.

Chapter 6

[xxviii] Cady, H. Emilie. *Lessons in truth*. Unity Books, Unity Village. 159.

[xxx] Nemeth, Maria (1997). *You and money: would it be all right with you if life got easier?* Vildehiya Publications, Sacramento, CA. 39

[xxxi] Wattles, Wallace D. (1910) (2007), *The science of getting rich: the proven mental program to a life of wealth*. The Penguin Group, NY, NY. 112

[xxxii] Ibid. 112.

[xxxiii] Fillmore, C. (1959), (1994). *Revealing word,* Unity Books, Unity Village, MO. 135.

[xxxiv] Ibid. 68

[xxxv] Ibid. 115

Chapter 7

[xxxvi] Fillmore, Charles (1936). *Prosperity*. Unity Books, Unity Village. 103.

[xxxvii] Nemeth, Maria (1997). *You and money: would it be all right with you if life got easier?* Vildehiya Publications, Sacramento, CA. 110.

[xxxvii] Wattles, Wallace D. (1910) (2007), *The science of getting rich: the proven mental program to a life of wealth*. The Penguin Group, NY, NY. 112.

[xxxvii] Ibid. 62.

[xxxviii] Nemeth, Maria (1997). *You and money: would it be all right with you if life got easier?* Vildehiya Publications, Sacramento, CA. 111.

[xxxix] Ibid. 113.

[xl] Ibid. 116.

[xli] Ibid. 117.

Chapter 8

[xlii] Fillmore, Charles (1936). *Prosperity*. Unity Books, Unity Village. 109

[xliii] Wattles, Wallace D. (1910) (2007), *The science of getting rich: the proven mental program to a life of wealth*. The Penguin Group, NY, NY. 46

[xliv] Ibid. 48

[xlv] Wattles, Wallace D. (1910) (2007), *The science of getting rich: the proven mental program to a life of wealth*. The Penguin Group, NY, NY. 46.

[xv] Ibid. 46.

Chapter 10

[xlvi] Friedman, David. (2005). *Is tithing for me? a practical exploration of tithing*. Middler Music Publishing, Inc. Norwalk, CT.

\ABOUT THE AUTHOR

Reverend Doris Hoskins was ordained a Unity Minister in 1994. She began her ministry by co-founding a church, High Country Unity, in Littleton, Colorado [now Unity of Littleton] with Rev. Scott Schell, where she served for five years. Called in 2000 by New Thought Unity in Cincinnati, Ohio to apply for the Co-Senior Minister position with Rev. Pat Williamson, she served at New Thought for eleven years. In March of 2012 she accepted the call to serve a new start up group, Unity of Northern Kentucky, in Fort Thomas, Ky.

Doris is the mother of three, and the grandmother of three beautiful granddaughters. She first walked into a Unity church in Fayetteville, AR in November of 1987 and Unity has been her spiritual path ever since. She is grateful to Rev. Gary Simons her first minister and Unity of Fayetteville for the important part it has played in her journey. She completed her Masters at Fielding University in Santa Barbara, CA in 2012 with a degree in Organizational Management and Development with an emphasis in Integral Studies.

Doris currently serves as a Minister at Large in the Greater Denver area.

While at High Country she designed and copyrighted the Harmony Pendant, an important symbol for our times, which she also now sells at various Unity churches and at www.harmonypendants.com she can be reached at doris.g.hoskins@gmail.com

Made in the USA
Columbia, SC
05 May 2018